Dmitri Bilgere has been involved in leading personal growth seminars since 1988. He has worked extensively with groups of men and women, teaching them the simple-but-not-obvious skills of life-success, relationship happiness, emotional prosperity and gender reconciliation. He has run seminars all over the United States, in Canada, England, and South Africa. His *Life Power Skills Seminar* and other programs teach important skills of life-success in a fun, experiential environment.

To get Dmitri's calendar of events, to get on his mailing list, or to order books and other products call 608-233-0881. Or write:

> **Life Power Skill Systems**
> PO Box 55094
> Madison, WI 53705-8894

You can visit Dmitri's internet site at
http://pobox.com/~LifePower
or email **LifePower@pobox.com**

What people are saying about
Beyond the Blame Game:

"A significant contribution toward ending the battle of the sexes.... invites everyone to understand that men and women have more similarities than they have differences."
—Bill Kauth, co-founder of *The New Warrior Training* and author of *A Circle of Men*

"Reading this book will create more compassion for both men and women....insights and information that will change the way you think and feel about the 'opposite sex.' A must read."
—John Lee, author of *The Flying Boy* and *Facing the Fire*

"*The* manual to help women understand men, and to help men understand women....made my relationships with men improve instantly and permanently....Buy it."
—Karen Krizanovich, relationship advice columnist for *Sky* magazine

"I definitely recommend this book. It's a provocative and articulate view on a subject which deserves wider attention. An important read."
—Harry Stein, author and columnist for *TV Guide* magazine

"It really opened my eyes. I thought I was in tune with gender issues, but this book made it clear how much I had to learn. Dmitri Bilgere introduces new ideas in such a way that not only can both women and men understand them, they also want to understand them. Very lucid and highly recommended."
—Leland Howe, best-selling author of *Values Clarification*

BEYOND THE BLAME GAME

Creating Compassion and Ending the Sex War in Your Life

For information, contact:
MPC Press
PO Box 55094
Madison, WI 53705-8894

ISBN 0-9613177-3-6

Printed in the United States of America

Contents

Acknowledgments

F EW worthwhile projects are accomplished without substantial help. I have been supported by a wonderful team in the writing of this book, and would like to acknowledge them now.

First I must thank my parents, John and Julia Bilgere, for their unwavering support. Thanks for being the perfect parents for me. I must also thank Dr. Roy Schenk, without whom I would never have even begun this project. I must thank my editor, Eric Pierson, for all his feedback and help, and the many others who made up my support team: Trisha McConnell, Roan Kaufman, Bill Kauth, Cliff Barry, David and Julie and Meleia Egger, Karen Krizanovich, Erva Baden, Mary Ellen Blandford, Bob Reed, Tom Daly, Jude Blitz, Craig Rypstat, Leland Howe, John Lee, and Joshua and Harry Stein. I also wish to thank the many others I am sure I have left off this list, without whom this book would never have happened. Thank you all.

As this book goes to press, I feel like I am letting my child out into the world for the first time. I am reminded of what Benjamin Franklin once said after publishing a piece of his writing: "I concluded to let my papers shift for themselves." So now my book is out in the world, and must shift for itself. I'm glad it has found its way into your hands. Thanks for reading.

Beyond the Blame Game

Chapter 1

Perspective

OVER the past few decades, dedicated women have brought a new perspective on women to our society. Meanwhile, men have not produced a new perspective on men. As a result, we understand only one-half of many of the dynamics between women and men. For example, we understand well how women are oppressed, but we know little about the oppression of men. We empathize with the sacrifices women make juggling a family and a job, but have little empathy for men who do the same. We read books and watch talk shows about how men don't live up to women's relationship expectations, but rarely talk about how women fail to live up to men's. We understand how women are disadvantaged in the workplace, but not how men might also be. This is not to say that all of women's problems have been fixed—obviously, that is not so—but the women's side, at this point, is far better understood than the men's.

When half of a dynamic is already understood, the task of reconciliation is to explain the less-understood perspective, and to show how that perspective balances, without invalidating, the better-understood side. Accordingly, we will start by examining the dominant perspective on gender issues our society has now.

Feminism has made us aware of how we see women: it has changed our perspective on women. Our culture now takes women's opinions about work and politics seriously. Today, more people than ever are sensitive to whether an attitude or statement might be considered offensive or inconsiderate by *any* woman.

We can see this change in attitude by reading some comics from the 1970s. Comic strips are, according to domestic violence researcher Susan Steinmetz, "a reflection of popular values,"[1] a barometer of our culture at large. Comic strip characters like Cathy Guisewite's *Cathy* no longer have any problems getting people to take women's ideas and women's careers seriously. In the 1970s, *Cathy* thought of herself as "just a girl with a job." Now, her career is never in question. Men used to refuse to call her Ms., insisting instead on Mrs. or Miss. In the 1990s, this is not an issue. Her boyfriend often used to be extremely inconsiderate and manipulative: "How am I going to get to know you," he asked, "if you won't sleep with me?"[2] Today, he's much more respectful of Cathy's feelings and experiences, saying things like "Please stay just as you are."[3] Even the lascivious General Halftrack in *Beetle Bailey* has been accused of sexual harassment by the women on his staff. The "ditsy broad" of the past is largely gone. Our society's perspective on women has changed.

But we still don't know much about the male perspective that balances the female. Women have articulated a new, more positive perspective on women. Not being men, they have not been able to articulate a new, more positive perspective on men—and it's not their job, anyway. Over the last few decades, limiting stereotypes about women have become less common— a women's place is no longer simply the kitchen—but only recently have men started examining the stereotypes which limit them. We still have male-only draft registration because our society considers men's lives to be more expendable than women's, and believes that because a few men start wars, other men—boys, really—should have to fight them. In divorces, women are still awarded sole custody of children eight times more than men are,[4] because many courts still believe that men are inferior as nurturers and superfluous as parents. These beliefs—that men are expendable, men are the problem, men can't nurture as well as women—are examples of stereotypes about men that our society has yet to address.

The task of creating a positive male perspective, and thus a balanced perspective on gender issues, is complicated by many people's belief that we already have a positive, compassionate perspective on men, so that nothing needs to be done. For example, a friend of mine recently participated in a panel discussion about men's issues, where he stated that there is a need for "safe emotional spaces for men." Listeners in the audience became angry, claiming that every place is already a safe space for men's emotions. My friend, who has worked with men's groups for many years, asked the audience, "Then why do you think you see so few men sharing their feelings? Is it because they feel safe, or because they don't feel safe enough? Just because some men have power in some areas doesn't mean all men feel powerful all the time." But the stereotype of men being always powerful and always safe prevailed in the room.

Because stereotypes about men, men's feelings, and the experience of being male in our culture have never been explored as thoroughly or as publicly as women's experiences have been, women have developed a perspective on gender issues, while men have not. We are barely aware of a male perspective on gender issues. What we have is not a neutral or balanced perspective; we have a female perspective. This is a problem because understanding only one perspective, be it male or female, keeps men and women stuck in conflict.

What is a Balanced Perspective?

Gender issues are *relationship* issues. As we will see, women tend to be our society's custodians of relationships. They think more about relationships, read more books and articles about relationships, and initiate more conversations about relationships than men do. As the relationship custodians, they have analyzed relationships, including gender issues, longer and in more depth that men have.

Because women have been looking at male-female relationships a lot longer and a lot harder than men have, our society has accepted the female perspective as "The Truth" about male-female issues. From advice columnists to authors of books about gender issues, women's perspectives are more accepted and more pervasive than men's.

Our society's reliance on the female perspective on gender issues has made it the *only* perspective on gender issues. In fact, a popular feminist slogan is "feminism is nothing more and nothing less than equality." The belief that feminism is the same as equality, and that any "feminist" opinion, no matter how outrageous, is the voice of equality, indicates that women's perspective is the only perspective on gender issues. This has happened because, while women were developing their perspective, men were not developing their own. Men are more likely to talk about work or sports than about relationships. Most men have *no* perspective on gender issues, so they have had to use women's, shrugging their shoulders in mystification about women's often-vocal dissatisfaction about relationships and work.

This hasn't worked well for men. While some of what feminists have said is absolutely accurate—men and women should, for example, have economic and political parity—some of what they've said is only accurate if it is balanced by a male perspective. Angry women have used the dictum "feminism equals equality" to get *anything* they say accepted as truth—including ideas that are vicious and hurtful. Men who have tried to support the women's movement have often been hurt by feminism's inaccurate and unflattering conclusions about men. It's hard for a man to feel good about himself while supporting a movement whose leaders say things like "Every woman's son is her potential betrayer, and also the inevitable rapist and exploiter of another woman."[5] Or this, from the editor of *Ms.* magazine: "I feel that 'man-hating' is an honorable and viable political act..."[6] Men who favor equality often want to support the women's movement, but it is a trap: a man who adopts a feminist agenda risks accepting angry women's rage at men into himself. That does not help men, and it does not create equality.

Because women never experience being men, and because both genders have a hard time believing that the other might experience some of the same pain they do, women are unable to do more than guess at what men's lives are like, or what a male perspective might be. Men, however, are beginning to develop their own male perspective. This emerging perspective will balance the female perspective and allow our society to move into an entirely new view on gender issues.

Equal Compassion

How can we tell when we are seeing with both a male as well as a female perspective? We are seeing with a male as well as a female perspective when we judge women and men with equal compassion. We are seeing with a balanced perspective when:

• We seek equally to explain the reasons behind both men's

5

and women's behaviors. We don't seek to understand one gender's behavior, while seeking only to punish the other gender's behavior.

• We care about and are considerate of *both* genders' emotions. We see both men and women as wounded, and seek to heal those wounds equally.

• We understand the emotional blocks that tend to hurt both men and women. We understand the shame that many men experience about being men. We understand that rather than constantly feeling shame, many men shut down emotionally and feel nothing at all. We learn to see the effects of this shame in male behavior.

• We understand that male-female relationships operate as systems of behavior, and we use this understanding when analyzing relationships.

• We have a knowledge of the stereotypes that hurt women, and a knowledge of the lesser-known stereotypes that hurt men. We act on this understanding when we make judgments about relationships.

Compassion is the thread that draws all these points together. We have to be compassionate to seek to understand, rather than to simply look for a "bad guy" to blame, label and punish. Developing a compassionate view of both men and women, a perspective that loves and supports both genders equally, is one of the first steps in creating gender reconciliation.

Seeing Men as Compassionately As We See Women

As a society, we usually judge women more compassionately than we judge men. Often, when a woman chooses to act in an illegal or anti-social way (by murdering her spouse, for instance), our society looks for a compassionate explanation: Did he beat her? Was he emotionally abusive? Did he have sex with other women? Generations of chivalry have taught us to automatically ask how a woman's negative behaviors might be understood compassionately.

Men's negative behaviors, on the other hand, are generally treated much more harshly. Women are consistently treated more leniently by the legal system than men are treated for the same crimes. The U.S. Department of Justice compared men and women convicted of similar crimes (homicide, robbery, assault, burglary, etc.). It found that men are 1.7 times more likely to be imprisoned than are women: 47 percent of men sentenced are imprisoned, compared with 28 percent of women. Women are 1.8 times more likely than men to receive only probation: 44 percent of women sentenced are given probation, compared with 24 percent of men. Furthermore, men and women imprisoned for like crimes are sentenced differently. On average, men are given sentences 40 percent longer than those given women.[7] Another example of our legal system treating women with more compassion than it treats men is an act of Maryland governor Donald Schaefer. He granted clemency to eight husband-killers, not all of whom seemed to be acting in self-defense. (One hired a hit man to kill her husband, and collected on his life insurance.[8]) Similarly, Ohio governor Richard Celeste granted clemency to 25 women convicted of assault or murder of their husbands or partners.[9] Yet, of these women, 15 said they had not been physically abused, two had killed husbands from whom they were separated, and six had premeditated the killing, sometimes talking about it for months before the actual murder.[10] It is indisputable that men, imprisoned under similar circumstances, would not get nearly the sympathy and compassion that these women have received.

Surely, many of these women were abused, but when was the last time you heard of clemency for the violence of a man because he had been abused by his wife? Although "battered woman syndrome" is becoming an acceptable defense for "treat[ing] violence-prone battered women as victims, not criminals,"[11] few people try to understand the violence that men do. No violence is acceptable, but there is clear evidence that violence done by women is "less unacceptable" than violence done by men. Our society looks to excuse, explain, and understand female violence much more readily than it does male violence. Our society has more compassion for women than it has for men.

The solution is not to see women with less compassion, but to learn to see men with more compassion. It's wonderful that we see women compassionately, and that shouldn't change. Society would benefit from seeing men more compassionately, as well.

Habits of Interpretation

We can use news stories involving men and women to examine our beliefs. Do you interpret male and female actions differently? Do you explain women's behavior more compassionately than you explain men's? We are socialized to interpret most of women's actions more compassionately than men's actions, and we don't usually notice this habit any more than we notice the air around us. This exercise will help you identify the differences in the ways you explain male and female behavior.

The following examples will put you in the same situation two times, once with a man and once with a woman. Watch for your automatic, intuitive, and emotional responses. Be aware of your body: do you feel more moved, or notice a more empathetic response for one gender or the other? Note the differences. This activity can show biases in our thought and behavior that have been with us for so long that they are no longer conscious.

1. a) You are the judge in a sentencing hearing. A woman

has been found guilty of murdering her husband. She has described in detail how horrible he was to her, and how, in her words, he "drove me to it." She looks pathetic. What kind of sentence might you give her?

b) You are the judge in a sentencing hearing. A man has been found guilty of murdering his wife. He has described in detail how horrible she was to him, and how, in his words, she "drove me to it." He looks pathetic. What kind of sentence might you give him?

What differences do you notice?

2. a) It is summer, and you are sitting indoors by an open window. You hear a man and a woman arguing outside. You look out and see the man strike the woman in the face. He hits her again, then kicks her. It looks as though he may strike her again. What do you think of him? What do you want to do?

b) It is summer, and you are sitting indoors by an open window. You hear a man and a woman arguing outside. You look out and see the woman strike the man in the face. She hits him again, then kicks him. It looks as though she may strike him again. What do you think of her? What do you want to do?

What differences do you notice?

3. a) You are the president of a large corporation. A male employee sexually harasses a female employee. How might you reprimand him?

b) You are the president of a large corporation. A female employee sexually harasses a male employee. How might you reprimand her?

What differences do you notice?

4. a) You are watching a TV comedy. A woman gets angry at a man and kicks him in the groin. What is your emotional response?

b) You are watching a TV comedy. A man gets angry at a woman and kicks her in the groin. What is your emotional response?

What differences do you notice?

5. a) You are watching a movie preview. One of the clips from the film shows a woman slapping a man in the face. What is your emotional response?

b) You are watching a movie preview. One of the clips from the film shows a man slapping a woman in the face. What is your emotional response?

What differences do you notice?

6. a) Fifty men are taken prisoner and killed by terrorists. What is your emotional response?

b) Fifty women are taken prisoner and killed by terrorists. What is your emotional response?

What differences do you notice?

After doing this exercise, you may better understand your different attitudes and ideas about men and women. Did you find that you were more likely to excuse, understand, and empathize with women's behaviors than men's? Did you find that women's pain was more easy to empathize with than men's? To treat a woman just as we would a man often means to treat a woman more harshly, while to treat a man like a woman often means to treat him more gently. There is a difference, and as long as this difference exists, we are not seeing with a balanced, equally compassionate perspective, and we will never truly end the war between the sexes.

The Reversal Test: Seeing Men As Compassionately As We See Women

The reversal test[12] is a tool we can use in any situation to find out if we are seeing men and women with equal compassion. For instance, if we read a newspaper story about a woman who shot her abusive husband, we can ask ourselves how we would respond if it were a story about a man who shot his abusive wife. If we see a woman slap a man on a TV show, we can ask ourselves how we would respond if it were a man slapping a woman. If our emotional reactions are about the same with either gender, then we are viewing men and women equally. If we are understanding about the woman's violence but appalled by the man's, or vice versa, we are not seeing men and women with the same perspective.

Let's try some reversals and see if our current view of equality is working. Would you consider it equality:

• if women criminals were imprisoned more, given less probation, and sentenced an average of 40 percent longer than men for similar crimes?

• if women died 7–10 years younger than men?

• if an operation analogous to the circumcision of young boys was routinely performed on baby girls?

• if 58,000 American women were killed in the Vietnam war, but only eight American men died?

• if men didn't have to fight in wars, while women did?

• if there were 24 women in prison for every one man in prison?

• if women almost always protected men, even if it meant risking their own lives?

• if special legislation were passed to protect men, even if women were 60 percent more likely to be victims of violent crimes?

If any of these inequalities worked to the disadvantage of women, women and men would protest until the inequalities were corrected. But in fact, because these inequalities happen to men, few women or men have done anything. This is not to say that inequality hasn't hurt women. Of course it has, massively, and it is absolutely essential that such damage done to women be corrected. And at the same time, it's worth noting that *our current perspective on gender issues does not allow us to see the damage done to men until we reverse the situation and pretend that the damage is being done to women.* Then the gender bias becomes evident. Inequalities that work against men, which our society would find totally unacceptable if they worked against women, are virtually invisible because we only see gender issues from a female perspective.

When we see gender issues with both a female and a male perspective, the reversal test always comes out equally—it doesn't shock us to see one gender in a situation any more than it does to see the other. You can use the reversal test in your life to determine the level of real equality in any situation, and to test your perspective on men and women.

Our society has a female perspective on gender issues. To have a balanced perspective, we must add a male perspective. The rest of this book will build that new perspective, and will explore the unexpected and wonderful effects of being able to see any issue from both a female and a male point of view.

What You Will Get From This Book

Reading this book will help you create compassion for both men and women. Compassion comes from understanding. You may wish to be compassionate for the other gender, but wishing alone will not make compassion happen. Until you understand their experiences as you understand your own, you will probably continue to feel about the other sex the same way you always have. Anger will stay anger, fear will stay fear, confusion will remain confusion.

When you are able to understand, however, you are able to be compassionate. You've probably had this experience many times already: for instance, have you ever been mystified by someone else's behavior, until you found yourself in exactly the same situation yourself? As a group leader I have sometimes been stunned at how poorly my co-leader seemed to be working with a participant. When I would step in to confidently take over, I would suddenly find out just how difficult this person's problem actually was, and feel *very* compassionate with my co-leader, whom moments ago I couldn't understand at all. Similarly, growing older often puts us into the same positions our parents were in, and we suddenly find ourselves with a new compassion for what they were going through when we were younger.

In the same way, men and women will develop compassion for one another as they grow to understand each other's experiences. This book is made up of the insights and understandings that groups of men and women I've worked with have discovered through trial and error. In a few hours of reading, you can learn what often took them months to discover.

If you are a woman, a compassionate understanding of both women's and men's behavior will dramatically improve your relationships with men. You will learn how blaming men for women's problems disempowers women, and learn how to be responsible for your relationships without feeling guilty about the relationships' problems. You'll learn how to not *have* to control men to get what you want in relationships, and you'll learn how to communicate so the men in your life can really understand you.

A woman who understands both the male and female perspectives has much easier, more balanced relationships with men. A woman who understands the male perspective is not angered or insulted by differences between women and men. To others, she appears to have a certain knack for getting along with men. She doesn't live her life defining herself as a victim of men, and she rarely complains helplessly about her relationships. She never asks, "Where are all the good men?" She has a male, as well as a female, perspective.

If you are a man, having a balanced perspective will keep you from accepting the blame, as a man, for the world's problems. It will be harder for people who are angry at men to "guilt trip" you by claiming, "This is what men always do to women!" or using other accusations of sexism. A man who knows that men don't really have "all the power" any more than women do, is not easily manipulated by people who imply that he should make restitution or apologize because "men have all the power." A man who understands that gender relationships operate as a system is not going to be manipulated by a woman who asserts that because men have all power over women, he must be dominating her and should back down in whatever conflict they happen to be in.

It is my desire and intention that the understanding you will get from this book will guide you toward compassion for the other gender, and build gender reconciliation in your life.

The Six Most Important Understandings

To that end, this book will explore the six most important understandings that I have identified in my years of working with men and women. Without these six most important understandings, men and women have conflict. With them, it is much easier to develop compassionate perspectives on and strong relationships with one another. We'll explore these missing understandings throughout the rest of this book:

The six most important understandings are:

• **Shame.** Men and women experience very different kinds of shame, and our lack of understanding of shame dynamics wreaks havoc in relationships. We'll look at how women have traditionally learned to feel ashamed about being incompetent, and at how men have learned to feel ashamed about the abuses men have perpetrated upon women and upon the world. We'll examine how this shame interferes with good relationships, and ways to identify and heal it.

• **The different ways in which men and women are empowered**. Men and women do not become empowered in the same way. We'll explore how a child growing up finds different "empowerment doors" open or closed, depending on his or her gender. You'll see how our culture makes it much easier for boys to become empowered around achievement, while girls are more often empowered in the areas of feelings and relationships. We'll examine how our general lack of understanding of these different areas of empowerment causes difficulty and confusion between men and women.

• **The system of male-female relationships.** Codependence theory and family roles therapy have taught us that relationships exist as systems to which both parties contribute, and from which both parties benefit. With the best of intentions, men and women very often create relationship dynamics that trap them into downward spirals of anger and fighting. You'll learn how to identify and stop these painful patterns before they destroy your relationships.

• **The dehumanization of men**. Men are one of the few groups that otherwise socially aware, equality-committed people still feel free to degrade and abuse. Stereotypes clump men into one "bad" being, and treat all men as the worst of what human beings can be. As long as the stereotyping of men is unexplored, men will remain dehumanized. Balanced, healthy relationships between men and women will be impossible. You'll learn to see the usually-invisible stereotypes that *de*humanize men, and how to keep them from interfering with your life and your relationships.

• **Violence.** The ways in which our society explains violence between men and women keeps men and women apart. We'll examine the fallacies in how our society explains intergender violence, and chart a route to creating a society made up of

relationships that are loving, supportive, and truly non-violent.
• **Sex.** Men and women have profoundly different experiences with sex and sexual availability. Sexuality, including sexual desires and fantasies, has long been shamed in our culture. You'll learn how to build better sexual relationships by increasing your sexual self-esteem and honoring your sexual style.

These understandings enfold together to create an *attitude* that automatically creates compassion and empowered relationships with the opposite sex. Like many life-changing ideas, these ideas are simple, but not intuitive. Once you understand them, you'll find them easy and natural to integrate into your life.

Generalizations and Stereotypes

This book uses generalizations, and it is important to understand their uses and limitations. For example, the statement that "people usually stereotype men as superior achievers and women as morally superior" might be casually dismissed as a generalization, as if the fact that the statement is general automatically makes it invalid, useless, and untrue.

People who are afraid of stereotyping others are often too quick to dismiss a useful generalization. There is nothing inherently wrong with making a well-informed generalization, if we bear in mind two things: First, the generalization may be unconvincing or just plain wrong. Examine the evidence for generalizations and make your own decisions. Second, a generalization becomes a stereotype when we apply it to individuals as a substitute for getting to know them. When generalizations become substitutes for actually getting to know people, then we are stereotyping, not generalizing. If I meet a woman and say "She must be like _____" because of some generalization I have made about women, I am stereotyping. There is no substitute for treating people as individuals. Discussing gender issues necessarily involves some generalizations and that's okay, as long as we know the difference between making a well-informed generalization and stating a stereotype.

Statistics

Statistics, which are often used as generalizations, are always a little bit tricky. Mark Twain said there are lies, damn lies, and statistics. (There are probably statistics to back that statement up.) What are we to think when statistics conflict, as they do in gender studies? We can and should ask questions about how data was sampled and compiled, the biases of the researchers, and how accurately the studied phenomena was reported.

Methods of sampling and biases of researchers can distort the very phenomena that research ought to clarify. For instance, a study of date rape[13] found date rapes in alarming numbers. However, the researcher's definition of rape was so broad that 43 percent of the women "raped" did not believe that they had been raped at all. Furthermore, the questionnaires "led" the women filling them out. Just as a salesperson creates an "atmosphere of yes" by asking questions that everyone answers "yes" to, this study asks questions that incrementally build a woman up to interpreting her sexual experiences as rape. This flaw, and other defects of the study (including the method of selection of women polled and the biases of the questions) makes this researcher's conclusions seriously questionable. Yet, because it is a "statistical fact," the supposed 25 percent incidence of rape or attempted rape on campus has come into general use by universities and national magazines, even though it conflicts with the U.S. Department of Justice's finding that the incidence of rape is decreasing.[14] "If you have to convince a woman that she has been raped," asks author Stephanie

Beyond the Blame Game

Gutmann, "how meaningful is that conclusion?" Statistics are not necessarily true merely because they are statistical.

Other statistics that have become common knowledge, such as the claim that "women make 69 cents to each man's dollar," turn out after inspection to be either wholly inaccurate or seriously questionable. Still, people often treat statistics as objective, eternal facts.

As an author, I can't easily ignore statistics, especially when they support my arguments, and when people I disagree with are using other statistics so effectively. Everyone who wants to persuade others quotes statistics when they support their ideas, so I ask you to take all statistics with the skepticism they deserve. I encourage you to look at statistics as the kind of thing that might be true, or that is sometimes true, or as a range of possibilities. Some statistics are more straightforward and objective, because they measure easily counted, concrete things. Little judgment is required, for instance, to compile statistics about on-the-job deaths. A worker either died or didn't. Behavioral statistics, on the other hand, are much harder to make precise. Make your own decisions.

It's Easier Than We Think

Women have been more diligent about developing and articulating their perspective than men have been about theirs. Women have insisted that men attempt to understand women's experience, while few men have asked women to understand men's. Unfortunately, however, understanding only one side of a dynamic seduces us into looking upon the side we understand as the blameless winners, while looking upon the less understood side as the guilty losers. Understanding only one side tempts us into the blame game. To the extent that this has happened between men and women, understanding only one side of the dynamic hasn't ended the gender war. Indeed, the

18

continued strife between men and women indicates that understanding only one perspective has only intensified the fighting.

To give up the blame game entirely we must understand both women's and men's perspectives. Only then will we be able to come to an entirely new place in our relationships with the other sex. To complete our understanding of men's and women's issues, this book is largely about the male perspective that balances the female. It is not, however, about men's issues in a vacuum; its purpose is to discuss men's issues as a step toward understanding the complex dynamics that exist between men and women. If I think the women's side of some dynamic has not been explored or articulated, I will go into it as well.

Fortunately, the job of reconciliation is easier than we might think. A large percentage of people already understand many women's issues, and many men's issues are such direct analogies to women's that, given a little new information, a compassionate understanding easily becomes available to us. Through learning to compassionately understand women's experiences, we have already developed the tools we need to compassionately understand men's.

For instance, the media's exploration of the difficulties women have mixing family and a career may have helped you to feel compassion for women who juggle a job and a home life. If so, when you learn that men who juggle work and family face the same dilemma, you will more easily feel compassion for them. Compassion is just a matter of noticing how men experience the same dynamics as women do, and letting ourselves respond to men's pain in the same way we would with women's.

I saw this recently when I was a guest on a radio call-in show. A woman called in about her experience with a man who abandoned her in a brutal, cruel manner. Her conclusion was that men were untrustworthy in relationships. It was easy to understand her pain and feel compassion for her. Several calls later, a man told an identical story about how he had been abandoned by a woman. I said to him, "You can probably understand what that woman caller is going though, can't you?" He admitted that he could. "And so, since you are experiencing that same pain yourself, you can probably be compassionate for her, can't you?" "Yes," he admitted, surprised by his own compassion. "And in the same way," I continued, "the woman who called in before, who was hurt by a man, can probably feel compassion for your pain, if she wants to. She certainly understands it well enough."

We can take the understanding of women's pain we already have and match it with an understanding of the other side, and vice-versa. When men and women develop this understanding, they can be compassionate towards each other, stop blaming, and end the war between the sexes. This is the kind of resolution that men and women are waiting for: a reconciliation that allows them to truly understand the other's perspective, without abandoning their own.

This book provides the necessary tools and understanding you need to finally end the blame game and to create a life in which both you and the other sex win. We will examine shame, relationships, power, violence, and sex, emphasizing the balance between the male perspective and the female, while adding previously unrecognized information about men where needed. Finally, we will explore how to integrate this new perspective, and how to live beyond blame, in every area of your life.

Chapter 2

Shame

THIRTEEN-YEAR-OLD Joey found a *Playboy* magazine on the way home from school, and his mother later caught him masturbating with it. "This is so bad!" she told him. "If you do this again you'll go to Hell." He felt so terrible that now, as an adult, he still feels ashamed about his sexuality, and has a hard time enjoying being sexual.

Fourteen-year-old Susan excelled in school, especially in math and the sciences. She usually set the curve, scoring so highly on tests that the other kids had a hard time getting top scores. One day she brought home a math test on which she got 100 percent, far higher than anyone else. Upon seeing the grade, her father was proud, but worried. He told her, "Always remember, Sue. Men don't like their women too smart. Are you scaring the boys away?" Susan was crushed, and learned that to be loved, she must not be "too smart." She felt so terrible that now, as an adult, she still feels ashamed about her intelligence, and has a hard time really enjoying the power of her mind.

What is Shame?

Shame is created whenever we are convinced, for any reason, to point to some part of ourselves and say, "That part of me is bad." Standing outside ourselves and pointing back in judgment is the essence of the shaming experience. In the above examples, Joey learned to point at his sexuality and say, "That part of me is bad." Susan learned to point to her intelligence and say "That part of me is bad." Both of them learned shame.

Shame starts in childhood. To small children, their parents are gods. In fact, some psychologists believe that our adult relationship with a God-figure is based on our early relationship with our parents.[17] Children are completely dependent on their parents for food, affection, happiness, comfort, and even their existence. They have no alternatives. Their lives are in their parents' hands, and on some level they know it. They also know they must maintain a connection with their parents to keep getting what they need to stay alive. Children will intuitively make this connection in any way they can.

Normally, when the parent accepts the child, the child learns to accept himself or herself. But the connection is broken when parents in some way send messages that the child hears as "You are bad" or "That part of you is bad," whether through direct abuse, neglect, or the myriad more subtle forms of abuse we've come to regard as normal. Messages like "Masturbation is evil. Never play with yourself again" or "Don't be too smart, or men won't love you," break the loving connection between parent and child.

To survive, the child must maintain a connection with the parent, no matter what. If the adult will not reconnect with the child, the child must reconnect with the adult. To do this, part of the child joins the parent in his or her own abuse and condemnation, abusing himself or herself the same way the parent does. When we learn shame, it is as if part of us leaves us, goes over to the abusive parent, and joins the parent in abusing us. *Whenever we are convinced or forced to join others in condemning parts of ourselves, we experience shame.* Because part of us has joined in the abusing, we continue abusing ourselves even after the original shamer is gone. Joey continues to feel ashamed of his sexual desire, even as a man. Susan continues to feel ashamed of her intelligence, even as a woman. We generate the condemning messages internally, and, like an unwanted house guest, the shame stays with us. In this way, shame is actually an internal process. In a sense, no one else can really shame us; it is something we learn to do to ourselves.

Shame for Girls

Boys and girls, and the men and women they become, learn to become ashamed in different ways. In the groups I work with, women often report that when they were children, authority figures told them that there were things they simply couldn't do because they were girls. This caused them to feel ashamed. They weren't allowed to help Dad or Brother tinker with the car; instead, they had to do the laundry. They couldn't join in when the men in the family went hunting because it was "man's work" and "no place for girls." Having to be dainty and lady-like taught them that women are frail and helpless. Well-meant dismissals such as "Don't worry your pretty little head about it," left them feeling stupid. When they looked for powerful or successful role models of women, they saw that almost every person who had political or financial power was male. All these factors conspired to teach girls that there was something inherently wrong with females that made it impossible for them to achieve as well as men did. Not long ago, there were almost no examples of women achieving in business or politics. It is understandable how a little girl, seeing that, might wonder about female inferiority in effectiveness, and might feel ashamed of being female.

Such shame is not always immediately visible. One friend of mine related a conversation she had with her mother. They agreed that they weren't interested in spending time with women, because women were boring while men were interesting. It wasn't until much later that she realized how her negative assessment of women also applied to her, and caused her to feel shame.

This shame is something women have to fight against in themselves. For many women this shame is always present, ready to tell them, "Of course you failed. Why don't you give up? You can't do it, anyway." Years ago, before there were examples of successful women in business and politics, giving up—if they ever tried at all—is exactly what many women did, without ever knowing why.

Confronting and overcoming this shame has been one of the accomplishments of the women's movement. While only a few short decades ago there were almost no female role models of "success," this is no longer true. Now, in every walk of life, a girl can find women who are successful and powerful. From doctors and prime ministers to astronauts and Supreme Court justices, women have taken on roles that even ten years ago were closed to them, and a generation ago were unthinkable for them to pursue. New laws and programs have forced changes in the workplace that guarantee women the equal right to strive for success. While there is still sexism in the workplace and in politics that women must overcome, the progress made in the last twenty or thirty years is staggering. A little girl can now easily find female figures to inspire her about her possibilities and opportunities for the future.

While there used to be major educational and professional bias against women, times have changed. According to Diane Ravitch, Assistant Secretary of Education at the U.S. Department of Education, girls have more of a future to look forward to than ever before. In 1970, 41 percent of college students were female. By 1992, 55 percent of college students were female. In 1970, women earned 14 percent of all Ph.D.s; in 1990 they earned 37 percent. In 1970, women received only 5 percent of all law degrees; in 1989, women earned 41 percent of all law degrees. In dentistry, women in 1970 earned less than one percent of the degrees awarded. In 1989, that figure had risen to 26 percent. Such an increase has occurred in medicine, as well. In 1970, women earned eight percent of medical degrees. In 1989, women earned 33 percent of all medical degrees. Notes Ravitch, "In every professional field, women have made large strides toward full equality, and in some cases—such as pharmacy and veterinary medicine—women have become the majority in what was previously a male-dominated profession."[18]

Clearly, a women's place is no longer simply in the home. Now, as one bumper sticker says, "A women's place is in the House. And the Senate."

Shame for Boys

Boys are socialized into a different kind of shame. Girls and women have traditionally been taught to believe they are defective in their ability to do things properly, which caused them shame. Boys and men, on the other hand, learn to believe that they are defective in their morality, and in their ability to relate, love, and feel emotions properly. This causes a very different but equally devastating shame for men.

In the groups I work with, men often report that, as boys, authority figures told them that they were bad, born trouble-makers, and naturally immoral. After all, as the saying goes, "Boys will be boys!" While the girls were "sugar and spice and everything nice," boys found out they were "slugs and snails and puppy dog's tails." (I remember as a boy thinking, "Why do I have to be the slugs and snails? Why can't I be the 'everything nice'?") One 14-year old boy I know says that "In school, girls are better than boys. The teachers always believe the girls, but almost never believe the boys." Boys get in more trouble than girls do. Of all special education students, 69 percent are boys, and boys are more often held back a grade than are girls.[19] They have a harder time sitting still, and often seem to learn better by doing, rather than by reading or listening. Instead of adapting to the different needs of boys, schools label them as trouble-makers, or hyperactive, or as having Attention Deficit Disorder. These labels teach boys what my young friend is learning: in terms of "goodness," boys are inferior. Such messages produce shame.

The men I've worked with further report that they often had to do the strenuous, dirty or dangerous work, such as changing the oil in the car, mowing the lawn, or shoveling snow, while their sisters got to stay inside. Having to be tough, uncomplaining high-achievers ultimately taught them that men are brutish and unfeeling, only caring about the ends, not about the means. And, when boys looked for powerful, happy, positive role models of men, they saw only tough, high-achieving superhero/killers, and a world in which men did most of the crime, violence, and abuse of women. All these factors conspire to teach boys that there is something inherently wrong with males that makes it impossible for them to feel, be sensitive, or relate as well as females do. It's understandable that a boy, seeing this, might wonder about male moral inferiority, and might feel an unspoken shame about being male.

Shame About Not Achieving Well Enough

Boys are subjected to massive and unrelenting pressure to perform and to divorce themselves from their feelings. A boy who is hurt is rarely told "It's okay to cry." Even if he is, so many other messages tell him that "big boys don't cry," that whatever crying he does is tinged with shame. More often, boys do as they are told: "Be a man." "Shake off the pain." "Be brave." "Pitch through your tears." "Don't be a girl." "Don't be a sissy." "What are you, scared?" Boys are rewarded for toughness, and punished for tenderness. This teaches boys to be ashamed of their feelings, and to divorce themselves from them. For boys and for the men they become, feelings get in the way.

Today there are more options for boys to feel and express their feelings than there used to be. However, our culture is still more sensitive to the messages we send about girls' feelings than we are to the messages we send about boys'. Even *Sesame Street*, the popular forward-thinking, anti-stereotyping children's show, treats female characters with more sensitivity than male characters. "We're immediately criticized if we make a female character the object of a joke," says former executive producer Dulcy Singer, "but we feel perfectly free to do that with our male Muppet characters."[20] Issues affecting girls and how they feel about women are still generally treated with more sensitivity than issues affecting boys and how they feel about men.

Shame about Loving "Wrong"

Not surprisingly, boys who are taught to repress their feelings grow up to be unfeeling in relationships. The "feeling shame" that boys experience leads directly to the shame men feel later in life around their intimate relationships.

Boyhood shame is compounded by all the messages which tell men they are bad at loving, and don't feel emotions properly. There is certainly no shortage of books about what is wrong with men in relationships. Consider the popularity of the books like *Men Who Can't Love; Why Men Can't Open Up; Cold Feet: Why He Won't Commit; Men Who Hate Women and the Women*

*Who Love Them; The Peter Pan Syndrome: Men Who Have Never
Grown Up; Successful Women, Angry Men; Women Who Love Too
Much; Smart Women, Foolish Choices;* and *Sexual Static: How Men
are Confusing the Women They Love.* For those who have somehow missed the books, it is a common topic on daytime
television talk shows. Men just do not love right: women, the
media, and a great number of men all say so. This constant
assertion creates shame in men.

In spite of all the hubbub about how men do not or
cannot share their feelings in relationships, men's lives pressure
them to ignore their feelings. Mother, father, family, bosses,
women—many people punish boys and men for feeling, and
reward them for performing. It is dizzying, then, for a man to
survive boyhood, having learned not to cry, to laugh at pain, to
give up what he really wants in order to succeed—in essence,
to destroy his own humanity—only to hear a woman tell him
"Open up! Show me your feelings!" Too late! He cannot get
to his feelings anymore, and he will need skilled help to find
them. It is a sad fact that boys hear the message "Close up!
Hide your feelings!" only to grow up to hear "Open up! Show
your feelings!" Most men become emotionally immobilized
by this double-bind, in which they are ashamed if they do feel
and ashamed if they don't.

With this in mind, we can understand a major difficulty in
relationships between men and women. Women demand that
men share their feelings, and men, ashamed, have no idea how.
This sometimes makes women so angry that they try to make
men share their feelings by applying shame. Rock singer
Madonna advises women to "make him express what he feels,
and then you'll know your love is real," as if he were holding
back his feelings simply to be irritating. When a woman tries to
shame or coerce a man into sharing his feelings, she compounds
his sense of being emotionally defective, and makes him shut

down even more. The woman stays angry, and the man stays withdrawn and ashamed.

This already-serious problem is compounded by something I have seen many times: When men who have been emotionally repressed for a long time finally get in touch with their feelings, the first feeling they experience may not the kind of loving, intimate feeling most women want to see. The first emotion many men feel is *anger.*

When a woman says to a man, "Tell me your feelings," she probably hopes to hear a tender "I love you," not a fierce "I'm really, really angry!" or a whining "I'm feeling really ashamed." Often, anger and humiliation are all a man has to share. Whether he chooses to share nothing at all or whether he shares the "wrong" feelings, people see it as confirmation that men do not experience feelings properly. Either way, a man is left feeling ashamed of himself.

While women get the message "You can't do things right," men get the message, "You don't feel properly. There is something wrong with the way you love. Your emotions aren't right." This is a devastating, deeply shaming message for men.

Shame by Affiliation

Men also learn shame from seeing shameful acts done by other men. Just as girls looked at women's lack of leadership and political power and concluded that women were naturally powerless, boys look at the violence and abuse that men commit, and conclude that men are naturally bad. This happens because of a process called *affiliation.*

We all have a tendency to affiliate ourselves with groups of people who are similar to us. In sports, for instance, when our team wins we feel happy, and when it loses we feel sad. We are affiliated with them, and what they do affects how we feel. We feel affiliated with our country, or with our ethnic group, or with the people of our class or race, or who live in our geographical area. As result of these affiliations, their behavior can affect us and how we feel about ourselves. We can be proud of our country, we can feel proud of our race or class, and we can be proud of the area in which we live, taking offense if people insult the people of our state or region. We can also be ashamed of what the groups we feel affiliated with do. Many people find this out when they discover they feel ashamed of some of their government's actions. Some white people feel guilty about what whites have done to people of other races. Some wealthy people feel ashamed of the oppressive actions of the rich. Our desire to be part of something bigger draws us into identifying ourselves with the people we are similar to, for better and for worse.

We also feel a natural sense of affiliation with our gender. Many of us have seen how easy it is for men and women to become polarized into groups which struggle against one another. When conversation turns to relationships or gender issues, suddenly the women band together defending womens' point of view, and the men band together defending the mens'. We naturally and unconsciously affiliate with other members of our sex. In this way, when girls and women see how women behave, they develop feelings about themselves as women. Similarly, when boys and men see how men behave, they also develop feelings about themselves as men.

Un-Role Models

Children learn about themselves from the role models in their lives, and their identities suffer when those role models are missing. While girls and women now have role models of powerful, struggling victims, boys and men see absent or "dead-beat" fathers, destructive male "heroes," and men hurting women and damaging the world. In the United States in 1994, there were more than 7.6 million mother-headed households with no father present, compared to 1.3 million father-only households and 25 million married couples with children.[21] This fatherless status is no small problem for millions of children, both boys and girls. Furthermore, in fatherless households, little boys are all too often told, "You have to be strong. You're the man of the house now." For a boy who needs to be "big" in such a family, feelings get in the way. Even at a young age, he will suppress his neediness and terror, and become an emotionless Little Man.

In families where the father is physically present, he is often functionally absent. He may be emotionally vacant behind the newspaper or in front of the TV, or he may be always away at work, supporting the family financially but never really *with* the family. Many of the men I work with say that their fathers were "there, but not really there." From this they learned that "men are absent," and "men don't give emotionally." Ultimately they may say, as a man at one of my trainings said, "I learned from my dad that the best way I could love my children was to stay away from them."

Shame about What Men Do

While girls and women see other women oppressed or overcoming oppression, boys and men see other men who *are* oppressors. They see corrupt men in business and government, repressing others to fulfill their own grandiose fantasies. They see emotionally absent and abusive men in relationships. They see men starting and fighting in wars. They see men committing most of the crime, violence, and atrocities. They see men raping, oppressing, and abusing women. They see men destroying the environment and poisoning "Mother Earth." Seeing what men do—and what *they*, by affiliation, are doing—compels men toward shame.

There are few examples of men really feeling, nurturing, having relationships they love, and being powerful men. There are few examples of men who are actually proud of being male. At the same time, there are many examples of men hurting women and damaging the environment. It's understandable that little boys, and the men they become, might wonder about male inferiority in morals and feelings. Just as it's easy for women to see women as struggling victims, it's also easy for men to see men as hurtful predators and abusers of women.

Sexual Shame

On top of all of this shame, our society and our upbring-ing shames sexuality in men and in women. Our culture teaches a growing boy to divorce himself from his sexuality—to desire sex, but to feel ashamed of that desire. Many girls, on the other hand, learn not to desire sex, to be ashamed of the minimal desire they allow themselves, and to be disgusted by male desires. Parents would worry if a teenage boy had no interest in "sowing his wild oats," yet at the same time they teach him to be ashamed of and to hide those very desires. When men talk about the shame they learned about their sexuality, they often say they were taught that "If you want to be lovable, you shouldn't want to do *that* to girls." To be good, and to stay connected with their mothers' love and approval—and, by extension, to stay connected with women's love and approval—boys often condemn the sexual part of themselves.

Sexuality embodies a wide range of desires, most of which our moralistic culture tells men they shouldn't have if they want to be "good" men. To be "good," a man shouldn't want sex without commitment, shouldn't want a variety of lovers, shouldn't want to be too experimental, shouldn't enjoy sex magazines or videos, and should "heal" (meaning get rid of) the "kinky" parts of his sexuality. All of these desires are routinely labeled by women in men's lives as "disgusting," "sick," or "perverted." To maintain their emotional connection with these women, men learn to be ashamed of themselves and to call their sexuality "bad." We will explore sexual shame and other sexual issues in more detail in Chapter 7. For now, we will simply note that our society encourages and forces men to split from themselves, and to call the sexual parts of their psyche "bad."

How Shame Has Affected Men

The Day America Told the Truth, the largest study of morality ever undertaken in the United States found that "in America, women are morally superior to men. This is true all across the country—everywhere, in every single region, on every moral issue tested. Both sexes say so emphatically."[22] This finding is far from trivial. Almost everyone emphatically believes that women are morally superior to men. It's easy to imagine that this belief could be just as shaming to men as the belief that "women can't be leaders" has been to women. But the belief that women are poor leaders is being destroyed: the same study concludes that "the implication, of course, is that women should be looked to for leadership in this country...."[23] Men's need to unceasingly and unfeelingly achieve, the lack of good male role models and the abundance of bad ones, the stereotype that men don't feel emotions properly, and women's dissatisfaction with men—all these factors teach men to be ashamed of their moral inferiority to women.

Men haven't been nearly as successful as women have been in overcoming shame. Shame still profoundly affects men in the areas where they are most disempowered: around feelings and relationships. This shame is something that men will have to fight against in themselves, just as women fought against their achievement shame. For many men this shame is always floating in their unconscious mind, ready to tell them, "Of course you messed up this relationship. Of course women are unhappy with you. Of course you are a perpetrator: look at what men have done. Why don't you give up on being a good person? Why don't you give up on being a loving father? Just go back to making money." Sadly, many men do give up on themselves as good, feeling people, without even knowing they are giving up. While women have healed much—though certainly not all—of their shame, men have healed hardly any of theirs at all.

The Unfelt Emotion

How can it be that people feel an emotion as powerful as shame, and not know it? Actually, most people have had the experience of "discovering" a feeling they didn't know they had. Many of us have realized that we've carried anger or grief we didn't know about. Most of us have experienced realizing how much we loved or cared for someone only when they have died, left us, or moved away. We spend so much of our lives involved in external activities that our feelings sometimes remain a mystery. This is especially true for men, whom society punishes severely for being in touch with feelings, and whom society rewards for ignoring pain and "getting things done."

Shame is a feeling that even many "emotionally literate" men carry with them, yet know nothing about. I felt ashamed of being a man for years, and never knew it. Shame is an emotion that by its nature stays hidden. We have to look for evidence of it in our other feelings, our beliefs, and our behavior. Grief, joy, anger, and even fear can be shared with a sense of dignity and pride, but shame compels us to hide, to crawl under a rock, to get away—to do anything but share the feeling with others.

Shame is a difficult emotion to pin down. Many people

respond to shame by withdrawing. For these people, the feeling of shame is the feeling of *nothing*. But just as other feelings we aren't aware of can affect our behavior and well-being, unfelt shame affects men. Men who go for years feeling little or nothing have often had their feelings extinguished by a heavy, wet blanket of shame.

Of Machos and Wimps

Much of the shame that men experience is about *being male*. A man who has learned to think of men as the primary cause of the world's problems, who has had an absent father, and who has seen men hurt women and damage the world, must distance himself from his maleness to avoid being a "problem" himself.

Men handle this shame in two ways. Some men handle their shame by not really being able to be *proud* of being men. They become "sensitive men," or, as they are often less-charitably called, "wimps." Other men repress their feelings of shame about being men. Because we can't repress one feeling without repressing them all, these men become unfeeling, dangerous, and "macho." Either way, shame prevents men from being whole and happy.

First, let's examine the so-called sensitive man, or "wimp." This man actively abandons his maleness in order to feel innocent, unaware of or agreeing with the shame-inducing messages he is giving himself about being a man. He gets a woman's approval by showing her that he is not like all those other men who abused her, but that he is different or special. This was my approach to women for many years: I got approval from some women, but I also became increasingly ashamed of being a man. Feminist men often seek women's confidence by saying, in effect, "You can trust me, I'm not like a man." This may be an effective method of getting female approval, but unfortunately it comes at the cost of their self-esteem as men.

These men experience pressure from women, men, and their own shame to disavow their connection to anything male. They find themselves continually called upon to "give things back" to women to make up for what men have done, as a way to prove that they are not victimizers, "like other men." For example, an angry woman recently demanded that I change my behavior to suit her on the ground that I was "acting like a man." This dynamic is easier to see when it is a little exaggerated; a male character in the cartoon *Dilbert* experiences a "guilt attack" when a female character tells him, "Males have been discriminating against females for a million years. Therefore, *you* must compensate *me* for past injustices." As the male in the comic says, "You know, for a ridiculous argument, it's nonetheless quite effective."[24] Because of their shame, "sensitive" men are often at a loss to respond to such accusations, and end up making compensation. If a man succumbs to the pressure to make restitution for being male, he accepts negative messages about his gender and becomes even more ashamed and "wimpy."

In spite of their professed commitment to equality, these men are still motivated to chivalrously take on the most difficult and dangerous jobs, and to make sacrifices to protect and take care of women, as a way of making up for what men have done. This doesn't so often take the form of opening doors for women anymore. More likely, they will go out of their way to make sure that women are in leadership roles, are never insulted or uncomfortable, and have preferential treatment in the workplace. For them, equality comes to mean taking care of women, and working hard at not being "like men."

Men can learn to see themselves as good people *and* men, not as good people *or* men. They can insist that others see them that way, too. When a woman tells me that I am different from other men, this "compliment" has an insult built into it. It presupposes that men, in general, are defective human beings, and tells me that I am miraculously exempt from this condemnation. Accepting such a "compliment" reinforces feelings of shame about being male. It has helped me to honestly tell such women that I *am* like other men in many ways, *and* that I am a good person.

Macho men

Let's look at the much-maligned "macho man." These men intuitively know that it is important for them to *be* male and to access their masculinity. However, their repression of their feelings keeps them from becoming mature men. Such men access masculine energy in an unfeeling way, and become "macho."

Some people dismiss "macho" guys as jerks, and have no desire to understand them. We all know what "macho" guys are supposedly like. They smash beer cans on their foreheads, drive big pick-up trucks, get rowdy, and are simultaneously abusive and attractive to women. (Many women want "real"— meaning fully male—men, and will take them in this form if they can find no other). Jungian psychologist Robert Moore calls them "men who are fundamentally immature," and says that "'macho' societies deny *men* their mature masculinity as certainly as they degrade women…"[25] The problem is not masculinity; the problem is that masculinity rarely gets a chance to grow up. As Moore says, "If you don't initiate the Warrior [the aggressive energy young men feel], that aggression energy in a young man is going to damage his community and probably himself."[26] With all the early shaming that boys experience, the lack of positive male role models and the surplus of negative ones, and the pressures to divorce themselves from their feelings in order to perform, men often stay stuck as "cruel and abusive boys….acting out their immature and grandiose fantasies."[27] This is a tragedy, not a defect of being male.

Identifying Shame

Shame thrives in the secret dark and withers in the light. Identifying shame for what it is, calling it out, and seeing it starts the process of healing. Remember, shame is the process of joining in our own abuse, of pointing at some part of ourselves and saying "That part of me is bad." To stop shaming ourselves, we have to first see exactly how we are doing it. We must identify our internal shaming messages.

To this end, the next two exercises are about identifying shaming beliefs. These exercises are for men, but women can do them, too. To learn how men are taught to be ashamed, ask yourself, "Do I expect these behaviors of men?"

Do you experience Male Shame?

- Have you secretly disagreed when hearing women complain about men, relationships and equality, but have for some reason not voiced your objections?
- Have you reflexively promised to stop behaviors because a woman calls them sexist or offensive to women?
- Have you sometimes not done things because you were afraid that women would call them sexist or offensive to women?
- Have you had difficulty looking people in the eye, or looked at the floor a lot?
- Have you found yourself trying to prove to women that you're not like other men?
- Have you believed that correcting the injustices women experience is more important than correcting those experienced by men?
- Do you often or usually feel nothing?
- Have you been more concerned about a woman's wounds

and disadvantages than about your own?
• Does wanting to have sex with a woman seem somehow disrespectful of her?
• Do you wish you masturbated less, wanted sex less, or didn't like sex magazines?
• Have you felt intimidated when women accused you of sexist behavior?
• Have you often felt inarticulate around women, especially attractive women?

Every "yes" answer is a sign of shame. It is also a sign that you are a normal man. Shame is a dangerous, hidden problem for men, and it damages their lives and their relationships with women.

What Do You Apologize For?

Another way to identify our feelings of shame is to answer the question: How do I apologize for being a man? Apologizing for being male only creates more male shame, yet most men apologize without even realizing it. Men apologize through small behaviors that they can learn to recognize.

Once again, women can play, too. To continue to build a female perspective, women can ask, "How do I apologize for being a woman?" Or, to build a male perspective, you can ask yourself if you have been trained to expect these forms of apology from men.

Apology takes on an almost humorous variety of forms. Here are some examples from my own life and from men I've known:

I apologize for being a man by...
...Giving in anytime a woman suggests that I'm being sexist.
...Always putting the toilet seat down.
...Not expecting as much sacrifice from my female employees

as from my male employees.

...Automatically assuming my wife knows more about parenting than I do.

...Opening doors for women.

...Taking on the task of healing women's pain.

...Thinking I must take care of and provide for women.

...Making a point of *not* opening doors for women.

...Paying for a woman's presence on a date by paying for the meal.

...Taking the difficult jobs.

...Letting my wife pick out my clothes.

...Risking my safety to protect women.

...Lifting heavy things for women even if I don't feel like doing it.

...Apologizing for or being insecure about my sexual performance.

...Feeling ashamed for liking sex magazines or videos.

...Being more concerned about offending women than about offending men.

There are many ways to apologize! Ask yourself now how you apologize for being your gender. You may be surprised at what you find.

Healing Shame

Whenever we split off a part of ourselves and say "That part of me is bad," or "That part of me is the problem," we accept shame into ourselves. The prescription for healing shame, for both men and women, is simple: Identify it. Examine it. Stop keeping it a secret; let others know what you are ashamed of. Understanding that shame requires pointing at part of oneself and saying "That part is bad" also gives people some immunity against taking on any more shame. Men and women alike can make choices about what they believe about themselves. In the same way that many women now refuse to feel badly about themselves as women, men can refuse to feel badly about themselves as men.

As we understand our shame, it loses its power. We begin to notice when we are shaming parts of ourselves, and naturally stop. As we come to understand the shame we carry, we are able to change our beliefs, our behaviors, and how we feel about ourselves. Shame about being male tells men there is basically something wrong with them because they are men. The release from such shame is like the removal of a thorn.

As we will see in the next chapter, male shame makes men powerless emotionally, just as female shame made (and often still makes) women feel powerless around leadership and achievement. Male shame leads men to accept abuse, to not fight back against unfairness, to do and feel things they don't want to do or feel. As men learn to stop pointing to their maleness and saying "That part of me is bad," they will become much freer and happier. As women come to understand male shame, they will be much less mystified by male behavior. They will not be tempted to get the men they love to "open up" by trying to get them to feel ashamed of the way men express their emotions.

Just as there is nothing inherently wrong with women, there is nothing inherently wrong with men. Our society can learn that maleness is not a disease to be eradicated. Men do not need to be cured. Men can identify the ways they have allowed themselves to be shamed, and can stop accepting shame about being male.

Beyond the Blame Game

Chapter 3

Power

W HAT'S important to men is often mystifying to women, and what's important to women is often mystifying to men. Men often cannot understand some women's powerful desires to get married or have children. Women often cannot understand why some men enjoy working on cars and other technical hobbies, or why they like hunting or football. Women often fail to understand some men's ideas about honor and duty, and the male sex drive is quite a puzzle. Men often can't understand a woman's need to talk about feelings or relationships. What is important and what is dismissable are often quite different from one gender to the other.

Understanding what the other sex wants is even more difficult because we often don't understand why we ourselves want what we want. A women may *say* she wants a sensitive man, then become obsessed with men who are insensitive and unavailable. A man may *say* he wants an assertive women, then pursue women who are distant and aloof. Our different needs and desires, along with our confusion about ourselves, make communication and understanding between the sexes difficult.

These differences can give the impression that men's and

women's value systems are in opposition. He wants to make love, she wants to be held. He wants to see how things go, she wants to get married. She wants to talk, he wants to do something. It seems as if men and women are on opposite sides of a paradox.

We Appear More Different Than We Are

My years of experience leading men's groups, mixed-gender groups, and even groups made up entirely of women has taught me that men and women are actually more alike than they are different. There are real differences, but men and women are not as different as we commonly believe.

Men and women grow up empowered in different ways. These different ways of empowerment lead us to have superficially different sets of value, and these values create different *perspectives* through which men and women see the world. Because of these different ways men and women tend to be empowered, we see the same world differently. When we understand the differences in male and female empowerment it becomes easier to see past those differences to the ways in which we are alike. Until we can understand the different areas of empowerment of men and women, we will continue to perceive many differences where few differences exist, and be aggravated by what actually are superficial differences.

"Empowerment doors" that are generally held open to boys tend to be closed to girls, and vice versa. Thus, a woman who wishes to excel in a traditionally male achievement area is likely to meet resistance when she tries to open the door. Furthermore, she finds she is often not taken as seriously as a man would be (thanks to feminism, this is changing). Men, on the other hand, often find that their choices and moral judgments about relationships, feelings, and sexuality, if they disagree with women's, are not taken seriously and are even derided.

In addition, the way our culture has examined men's and women's power has hurt men. Although the ways men are empowered have been extensively discussed, the ways women are empowered have not been. The result has been that men are being called upon to give up their special privileges, but women are not being called upon to give up theirs. For this reason as much as any other, men have resisted women's calls for "equality."

Dualities and Paradoxes

To understand male and female empowerment, it helps to understand dualities and paradoxes. Dualities are paired opposites which are defined in terms of one another. Outside and inside, good and evil, up and down—all are paired opposite dualities. They are defined in terms of one another—"outside" only makes sense in relation to an "inside;" "good" only exists in relation to "evil;" "up" can only be defined by its relationship to "down."

People usually like to know where they stand on dualities. We tend to pick sides and try to eradicate darkness so there will be only light, or destroy evil so there will be only good. It is hard for us to see that dualities go together, and that trying to get rid of only one side is like trying to destroy "down" so that only "up" remains. Because paired dualities are defined in reference to each other, they need each other to be what they are. Philosopher Alan Watts says that "to see life whole is to understand these opposing qualities as essential to its existence."[28] And, as we will see, to understand men's and women's relationships requires us to understand the dualistic kinds of power they often have.

Another word for "duality" is "paradox." A paradox exists when two things are true that contradict each other, or when two things that are both true are as different as any two things can be. White and black are as different as two colors can be, yet they both exist. Going up is as different as can be from going down, yet both up and down exist. Good and evil both exist, at least as concepts, yet they are in dualistic opposition. Each of these dualities is paradoxical.

There is some evidence that the Universe itself is essentially paradoxical. Light, a basic building block of the universe, can be either a wave or a particle, two opposite states, depending on your point of view. Light is a paradox. And life and death are as paradoxical as any two states can get.

People are also more paradoxical than they usually care to admit. Most people see consistency as strength and inconsistency as weakness, so our internal paradoxes, which make us appear inconsistent, can be hard to admit. Yet they are there, if we know where to look. For example, people often describe their paradoxes when they talk about themselves: "On the one hand," someone might say, "I want to not eat sugar, and lose weight. On the other hand, I want to lose control and eat an entire chocolate cake!" These two desires, the "one hand" and "the other hand," are paradoxical. They are completely opposite, yet both exist inside the same person.

Almost every desire we have is in some way paradoxical: Part of me wants to have discipline, and get up early to work out. Another part of me wants to sleep in, eat whatever I feel like, and never be able to touch my toes again! There are also paradoxes in relationships between men and women: On the one hand, men and women love each other and spend their lives looking for ways to share that love. On the other hand, the sexes seem to be at war. The internal struggle between paradoxical desires is often called the struggle for "self-control." Our conflicting desires show our paradoxical nature.

Our complaints about our lives are also paradoxical. "I want to get more work done," we might say, "but something always gets in my way." This "something" is the usually unconscious part of ourselves that does not want us to do more work. One part of us wants us to move forward, another part holds us back. When Mark Twain says "One is not wholly displeased at the failure of a friend," he meant that one part of us wants to see our friends succeed, and there is another, paradoxical part of us, which secretly enjoys seeing him or her fail. Twain recognized that in each of us there are dual desires that are often in opposition, and that human beings are made up of many paradoxes.

The Paradox of Men's and Women's Power

Paradoxes are important to men and women because there is one paradox that defines and structures much of how men and women are socialized, how they are empowered, and how they interact with each other. This is the paradox of "goal orientation" and "feeling orientation." The two sides of this paradox exist in all of us, but our socializing trains us to see ourselves more in one side or the other, depending upon our gender.

Let's look at how the two sides of this paradox are empowered differently in males and females. Our society empowers assertive, goal-oriented behavior in men. Goal-oriented people set a goal and move toward it come Hell or high water, no matter what the cost to self or to others. Goal-oriented people are concerned with changing the external world and getting the job done. The goal may eclipse all other considerations. Men who are locked into the goal-oriented mode will do anything to reach the goal, even if it requires not taking care of themselves, ignoring their lovers or families, lying, cheating, and paying no heed to their own feelings or to the feelings of others. For goal-oriented people, their value to society and to themselves is based on achieving the goal.

Morality or even basic fairness can go out the window. The end is all-important, and the end justifies the means.

People who are empowered in the goal-oriented mode have an easier time getting power in the external, work-a-day, dog-eat-dog world. The goal-oriented mode is the mode used in most money-making, political, and business activities. Women, trained to be feeling-oriented, have been kept out of and oppressed in business and politics, the traditionally male achievement areas.

Men are society's judges of how well a job is completed, and they have often been quick to tell women workers they aren't doing the job well enough. Men are society's goal-oriented experts, so society has come to see men's ideas about work and achievement as better than women's ideas. *The ability to be obsessively goal-oriented is the basis of male power in the achievement-oriented realms.*

Feeling-oriented behavior, on the other hand, is concerned most with how an activity is gone about, and less with whether the goal is completed. The feeling mode emphasizes how relationships are maintained, how people feel about what is going on, taking care of people, and doing the "right thing." I once worked in a cooperatively-run business in which 90% of the workers were women. Making sure that everyone felt okay about a process was more important than getting the job done quickly and effectively. Women are usually more socialized than men into the feeling-oriented mode. Women are more likely to get their sense of self-worth from how they go about doing things, rather than from what they get done. They are more likely to be concerned with what is going on inside. Women are more likely to be concerned with maintaining relationships and fairness than with getting the job done. For women, the means are more likely to justify the ends. *The ability to be obsessively feeling-oriented is the basis of female power in the feeling and relational realms.*

We all have both sides of this paradox within ourselves, and a healthy person can be either goal-oriented or feeling-oriented, depending on the needs of any situation. Unfortunately, during our socialization we tend to be encouraged in one mode and discouraged in the other, depending on our gender. Men and boys are encouraged into the goal-oriented mode and discouraged in the feeling mode; girls and women are more encouraged in the feeling mode and discouraged around achievement. This creates many of the perceived differences between men and women.

Just because men tend to be pushed into the goal-oriented mode doesn't mean that men can't be feeling-oriented as well, and just because women are pushed into the feeling-mode doesn't mean that women can't get things done. I know some very goal-oriented women and feeling-oriented men, and plenty of people who can go back and forth as they desire. Generally, though, a man's feelings are more easily dismissed, and a woman's achievements are more easily dismissed.

Socialization

Socialization does not take an individual's loves, desires, or talents into account. Our self-esteem will always be tenuous if it depends on living up to some externally imposed standard of what we ought to be. This is equally true for goal-oriented men as for feeling-oriented women. Being pushed into goal-orientation or feeling-orientation creates much of the trouble between men and women.

And our socialization does push us. Boys are much more likely than girls to be punished for having feelings (with the exception of anger, which helps them to get things done). As we noted before, a young boy who bursts into tears is typically told to grow up, to not "be a girl," to stop whining, or the

49

ever-popular "Be a man!" Women get this particular kind of wounding in a much smaller dose.

Conversely, young girls are much more likely than boys to be punished for getting into the goal-oriented realm. Girls who elect to be tomboys are generally not so much encouraged as endured by their elders. Displaying feelings is okay for girls, with the notable exception of overt displays of anger. They may well be told, however, that it's okay to "go and have a good cry."

In summary, males and females generally are socialized into different areas of weakness and different areas of strength, which creates a greater sense of alienation between the genders than necessary. Males are pressured more to conform to an achievement-oriented success ethic, and repressed in their feelings, while females are pressured more to conform to a feeling-oriented "good girl" ethic, and repressed in their desires to achieve. Men as a group are more encouraged to feel powerful in business, economics, politics, and getting things done, while women as a group are more encouraged to feel powerful in anything involving feelings, be it relationships, socializing children, or judging the quality of men's feelings and motivations.

Looking for Women's Power in All the Wrong Places

The women's movement has exposed the special privileges and powers that goal-oriented men often enjoy. But what about the special privileges and powers that feeling-oriented women often have? Our society is starting to recognize that women are far from powerless, but there is still a long way to go before we are as conscious of the power socialized to women as we are now aware of the power socialized to men.

When social researchers have looked for evidence of female empowerment, they have looked in the same places we look for male empowerment: the goal-oriented economic and political realms. Finding few empowered women there, they have decided that "men have all the power," and "women are powerless." (These researchers ignored the fact that they also found very few empowered men. There just aren't that many politically or economically powerful *people*.) The goal-oriented areas are the least empowered areas for women, so of course it has appeared that women are completely disempowered. Because researchers have not looked anywhere else for evidence of women's empowerment, their conclusions about women's powerlessness have been widely accepted as true. Looking for women's empowerment in all the wrong places has fed the idea that men have all the power, and that women have none.

There are other reasons why women's power is hard to see. Women's power is more subtle and often less visible than the power society usually gives men. In addition, our society has a taboo against acknowledging many manipulative female behaviors, which creates a selective inattention toward the power usually granted to women. In our culture, it is acceptable to talk about the manipulative behaviors of men toward women, but it is virtually taboo to talk about women's manipulative behavior toward men. Discomfort is the natural consequence of breaking a taboo. Therefore, many men feel as if they are complaining, or being anti-woman, if they explore how women might manipulate men, or how women might be powerful. Other people, both men and women, feel angry when men talk about their experiences of powerlessness, because this violates the taboo against men complaining. Right now, you may be feeling as if there is something wrong with discussing women's power. Because of your socialization to not acknowledge women's power, you may find yourself dismissing women's areas of empowerment as unimportant. They are important. Recognizing women's empowerment does not put women down nor minimize women's pain. It simply helps us see the unexplored half of our society's power-dynamic. We must look at female empowerment if we truly wish to see men and women equally.

Shame Power

In contrast to the extensive research about women's disadvantages, the areas of women's special privilege and empowerment have barely been looked at. Still, they are intuitively familiar to us. Men have allowed women to be the experts at relationships. Women have controlled the home and the socialization and nurturing of children. Women often have the power to confer praise or moral condemnation on men (as in "female moral indignation"), a power men rarely have over women. The popular saying, "Behind every successful man is a woman" refers not only to the support women provide to men; it also recognizes that women's influence is very real, despite its subtlety and frequent invisibility to anyone outside the family. Angry women claim that this is a position of powerlessness for women, and it may be, as long as our definition of power includes only goal-oriented activities visible to the external world. However, it is also true that as a puppeteer stands behind the puppet, some women stand behind their men, powerful in a different but no less effective way than men.

It is a sad experience of many men that they cannot stand up to a woman's moral indignation and judgments about them. How many of us know men who are largely controlled by their mothers, wives, or girlfriends? How many of us have heard fathers say "whatever your mother says is fine"? (One man I know calls his wife "the boss.") How many of us have seen men crumble before accusations of sexism or misogyny? These are all examples of women's socialized power to control men's behavior by judging men and men's motivations. These controls can completely dominate the feeling and relational life of a man whose own power is limited to goal-oriented achievement.

Let's look at how this works. When an angry woman attacks an ashamed man about male sexuality, about men being unfeeling, about men abusing women, or about any other male "crimes," there is often an ashamed part of the man that agrees with her. This part believes that she is right, and agrees that maleness—especially *his* maleness—is bad. When a woman attacks him, this part of his psyche joins in his own attack. He has no defense from his own shame, and can therefore be easily manipulated by any woman who can press his "male shame" button. He is willing to keep quiet or change his behavior to stop the attack, because his inner agreement with her—his shame—is so painful.

Male emotional helplessness before angry women happens so regularly that most men don't notice it. It's simply part of the way life is. For example, one sunny August afternoon, several hundred people attended a "New Age Relationships" festival at a local city park. About 20 people attended a workshop about men's feelings of helplessness and emotional powerlessness. The audience listened quietly, until the only woman there interrupted the presenter.

"The fact that you guys think that you have anything to complain about is obscene," she said. "You guys always had everything, and you still do. If you want to experience suffering, try being a woman in this world of yours sometime. It's just disgusting that you think you're oppressed in any way. Men like you have exactly the kind of attitude that hurts women even more. It's disgusting. You should be ashamed of yourselves."

The 19 men were silent in the face of this accusation. Even at a workshop on men's emotional powerlessness and shame, no man was willing to risk being the focus of her attack by speaking out.

Similarly, I once saw a play about men's issues. The lively and pleasant discussion afterward was completely destroyed by one woman's shaming abuse of the men there. "You men have no right to think you have issues," she said. "Women have been slaves of men for thousands of years. I'm sorry, I just can't be too compassionate for the problems of the slave holders." If an angry man spoke like this about women at a similar women's event, he would probably be asked to leave (and even be told where to go). The men, however, were silent in the face of this woman's critical judgments of male feelings and experiences, and I detected a slight hanging of many of the men's heads. Because of their shame about being men, they could do nothing but wait submissively for her to stop.

As another example, a friend of mine has a daughter serving in the armed forces in Korea. One night, she went to a bar with a Korean man. An American serviceman, who happened to be black and twice her size, started berating her for associating with a Korean. It looked like things might get ugly. Then, my friend related with pride, her daughter started shaming the black man. "How can you be down on another race, after all the racism blacks have experienced? That's really horrible! Shame on you!" The serviceman stopped in his tracks, and apologized meekly.

Whether or not she should have used shame to stop him is moot. The point is that if a man had tried to do what she did, he might well have had his face punched in. Because she was female, she had special privilege to shame this man.

A male friend of mine recently experienced a similar dynamic. He was walking down the main street of our town with a group of men, when a well-dressed teenage girl asked them for some money. This kind of thing is typical in our city, and when they refused to give her money, she began to yell at them, cursing and calling them names. Said my friend later, "It was incredible. If a man had yelled at a group of large men like us in that way, he would have gotten the crap beaten out of him. No man would have talked to us like that and gotten away with it. As it was, she was able to get away with yelling at us as much as she wanted, just because she was a woman." Certainly no violence is appropriate—and just as certainly this woman was free to abuse a group of men because of her gender.

Consider a man and a woman who are having a fight—about anything. At some point in the discussion, she accuses him of oppressing her: "This is just what men have been doing to women for thousands of years!" Ashamed, the man backs off, withdraws, and gives in. A woman's ability to manipulate male shame has scored another victory. Calling a man "disgusting," "insensitive to women," "like other men," or "misogynist" to shame him into compliance are other examples of female moral feeling-oriented power, which women sometimes use to control and manipulate men.

Women have often told men that men do not relate well enough, that they just do not love right, that men do not open up right, and that all men want is sex. Men who refuse to alter their behavior discover that some women will try strenuously to get them to feel guilty or ashamed. Because socialization has cast women in the role of society's feeling-oriented experts, both men and women have come to see women's ideas about relationships and feelings as better than men's.

Ending the Battle Over Who Has it Worse

It is still debatable whether the empowerment women receive is equal to, less than, or greater than the empowerment men receive, but I have little interest in this debate. Battling over who has it worse and who has it better does not facilitate gender reconciliation. The sooner everybody realizes this, the faster gender reconciliation will proceed. Fighting about who has it worse and who has it better only draws the battle lines more clearly and makes us appear even more different from each other. Men and women alike have deep wounds that need healing. Arguing over whether women have it worse and men have it better, or vice versa is simply a battle I don't want to fight.

Nonetheless, because the way men are empowered has been so well explored, and because the way women are empowered is so poorly explored, our culture has come to believe that men have all the power, in all situations, always, and that women are always and forever powerless victims of men. The quest for sexual equality, then, has become a demand for men to give up their special privileges, while women give up none of theirs. As one feminist put it, the fight for equality is for "equal rights for 51 percent of the population."[30] Equal rights for 100 percent is vastly preferable, and will only come about when we can see with both female and male perspectives.

There are at least three compelling reasons to explore how power in the feeling-oriented and achievement-oriented realms affects men's and women's relationships. The first reason is to foster more harmonious relationships between men and women. When we better understand the outlook of the other gender, we can more easily see each other with compassion. When we understand how the other gender is socialized, we are better able to see them as human beings.

A second reason is for equality: the ways women tend to be empowered in our culture are much less visible than the ways men are. This has created a situation in which men are called upon to give up their special privileges in the name of equality, while women have not been called upon to give up theirs. Much of men's resistance to the women's movement comes from men's intuitive understanding that men do not have all the special privileges. As long as women ask men to give up their special privileges while women don't give up theirs, men will resist. Understanding how women tend to be empowered, as well as how men tend to be, allows us to create real equality for everyone.

A third reason is that our society's ignorance about the empowerment of women hurts men. When people see men as all-powerful, men get shamed and blamed unjustly. If we are to see in balance, we need to understand the empowerment of both men and women.

Just as empowering women has meant breaking down the barriers that kept them from achievement-oriented power, empowering men means breaking down the barriers that keep men from being powerful with their feelings and in their relationships. When men understand the dynamics of women's power, they can learn to stop modifying their behaviors for fear of shame or female moral indignation. Men can refuse to be shamed into silence. Men can make their own decisions about how well they function in their relationships, how committed they want to be, and the value of their sexual desires. Instead of allowing women to be the custodians of their feelings and desires in relationships, men can take responsibility for their relationships. Men can decide for themselves how they should feel, and not automatically change their behaviors whenever some women might consider them disgusting, insensitive, or "just like a man." Men do not need women's approval to feel good about themselves, just as women do not need men's approval to be successful.

Men and women who understand the power dynamics in their relationships are no longer slaves to those dynamics. More and more women today don't want to control men any more than today's men want to control women. Men and women who understand the male perspective allow love, connection and real intimacy to grow.

When we understand the empowerment of both men and women, it becomes easier to see that, as people, men and women are in the same boat. As we understand male and female power, we can end the war between the sexes.

Chapter 4

Relationships

WHEN we play the blame game, we look for innocence and guilt. Our upbringing trains us to be obsessed with right and wrong. We learn to see relationships in terms of victim and persecutor. In any conflict in a relationship, one side has to be wrong, and the other side has to be right. Either men are at fault, or women are. Either it's the husband's fault, or the wife's. Rarely do people depart from the right/wrong, victim/persecutor model of interpreting relationships.

It seems to be easier to redirect blame than it is to stop blaming. Feminism, for instance, has made such a switch. Historically, women were conditioned to blame themselves for the abuse or disadvantages they experienced. Until recently, for example, women who could not get jobs, or who watched as men were promoted ahead of them, were encouraged to feel that they themselves were not good enough, and that their defectiveness was the reason for the discrimination against them. Now radical feminism has performed a complete 180° reversal: deciding that if women need not always blame themselves, they should always blame...men!

Some angry women claim that women are always

and forever victims of men and of what men have done to the world. For example, Andrea Dworkin says that "Under patriarchy, no woman is safe to live her life, or to love, or to mother children. Under patriarchy, every woman is a victim, past, present, and future."[31] Occasionally, an angry man declares exactly the opposite, that women are the perpetrators who, through their manipulation of socialization and sex, "catch, control, and exploit a world of gullible, naive, male slaves."[32] Taking such extreme black-or-white positions is often easier than acknowledging that the relationship system between men and women hurts us all, and that the truth might lie somewhere besides one extreme or the other.

Many people hold a similar all-right-or-all-wrong attitude in issues of race. For example, in 1992 four white Los Angeles police officers were acquitted of using excessive force on Rodney King, a black man, even though the severe beating was captured on videotape. This jury verdict and the riots that broke out in response to it provide other examples of people's inability to see any middle ground in a victim/persecutor relationship. People's opinions about the riots commonly fell on one side or the other. Some said that blacks are victims of a system that crushingly oppresses them. According to their argument, the "not guilty" verdict in the Rodney King case told blacks that nothing they did mattered: even if you have a videotape of the police beating you, the system will say it never really happened. This helplessness and rage, some say, burst into a completely understandable violence.

The opposite opinion focused on the violence against innocent people, the killings, and the methodical gang looting and arson that became an opportunistic part of the riots. "They're just taking advantage of the situation," these people said. "It's not about injustice."

In fact both sides could easily be right. Yet some people

seemed stuck on the "rioters are perpetrators" side of the argument, while others seemed equally stuck on the "rioters are
victims" side. It was difficult for people to see any middle
ground, to see that both sides of this argument could easily
have been correct.

As actress Geena Davis says, in our society "you have to be
black or white. Nobody wants to live in the gray areas or the
very, very colorful areas."[33] This chapter is about learning to
live in the colorful areas of possibility and understanding that
appear when we understand more about how relationships work.

Fix the Problem, not the Blame

W. Edwards Deming, the business consultant whose ideas
revived Japan's economy after World War II, said that 85
percent of problems are caused by the system that management
sets up, and that only 15 percent are caused by the workers
who participate in the system.[34] Eighty-five percent of the
problems that are blamed on people, then, are actually
problems with the system. Deming dealt with dysfunctional
systems in the business world, but because people tend
to recreate their family systems in other areas of their lives,
business is a reflection of family. In dysfunctional systems, the
biggest problems are the inflexible roles that the system
designates people to play, not the people themselves.

Deming's "quality improvement" ideas for business systems
make a lot of sense for relationship systems, too. "Once people
recognize that systems create the majority of problems, they
will stop blaming individual workers," claims one quality
improvement manual. "They will instead ask which system needs
improvement, and will be more likely to seek out and find the
true source of the problem."[35] This is exactly what we need to
do in the system of male-female relationships. As Sean Connery's
character says in the movie *Rising Sun*, we need to "fix the

problem, not the blame."

Yet it is individuals who get blamed, as if they are exclusively at fault. For instance, in a dysfunctional family system, the child who has been cast in the family's scapegoat role is seen as the problem, rather than a symptom of a larger problem in the family system. Just as a dysfunctional family often casts one child in the role of the scapegoat, codependent couples often cast one member as the problem, rather than seeing his or her role as a symptom of problems in the relationship. All too often, one partner is blamed as the all-powerful perpetrator, while the other partner is disempowered in the role of the innocent but helpless victim.

This is important to men, because it is usually men who are cast in the one-sided role of the evil perpetrator. Even though perpetrator/victim generalizations in adult relationships also hurt women by reinforcing their beliefs in their own powerlessness, women are not readily identified as part of the problem, either by "helping" professionals or by society at large. A woman may believe she has no choice but to stay in (and reinforce) a relationship that hurts her, and she will always receive sympathy as the victim. The man, however, will always get anger and shaming as the perpetrator. Until the system of the relationship is addressed, its patterns will never be broken.

It is equally important for women to recognize relation-ship systems, because being seen as a victim in such a system is ultimately disempowering. As long as women believe that men are the problem and that women have nothing to do with their lot in life, there is little they can do to change their own lives but try to change *men*—through shame, blame, and manipula-tion. This doesn't work either, because you really can't make someone else change. When women (and men) see the system of male-female relationships, they can learn to stop being victims by changing their own behavior, rather than by trying to change men.

In the rest of this chapter we will examine relationship systems, with an eye toward understanding the types of systems that exist between men and women. We will start by examining some relevant systems that have been well-explored by psychologists: family role systems and codependent relationship systems.

Family Role Systems and Relationships

Sharon Wegscheider-Cruse is one of the pioneers of family role system therapy. She initially worked mostly with families of alcoholics, and discovered that people in families operate as a system. The more flexible the system, she found, the healthier the family. The more rigid and confining the system, the more dysfunctional the family. We will apply this same idea to men and women in two-person relationships.

Whenever people come together and relate to each other over a period of time, systems develop. In the family, this system is run by what Wegscheider-Cruse calls the *family rules.* The family rules "determine the functions of each person, the relationship between persons, the goals toward which they are heading, how they intend to get there, and what will be required and forbidden along the way."[36]

Wegscheider-Cruse uses the metaphor of a mobile to describe relationship systems. "Let us say that you have a mobile with five or six beautiful butterflies, all of different sizes, suspended by strings from three sticks. The butterflies can represent the family members, and the string and sticks the family rules. The whole thing has been very carefully designed to keep its equilibrium. If a puff of wind hits it, it responds immediately by rocking and twisting wildly, but then slowly it brings itself back into quiet balance."

This model gives us a visual way to imagine the way most

relationships work. People in relationships move together, connected by the sticks and strings of the relationship system. One part of the mobile doesn't "victimize" the other part; the whole thing is tossed about by the changing winds of life's events and circumstances. Like a mobile, our family relationships and our personal relationships are systems.

Specific Relationship Roles

The systems approach works well for family therapists, who see that family members, especially children, get pushed into different roles to maintain the family system. One child may be the hero, whose role is to fix everything and everybody. Another may be the rebel whom everybody can blame for the family's problems without having to look at real issues that might crack the family apart. Another might be the humorous clown who helps the family laugh and let off steam, while another, the shy "lost child," withdraws to stay out of the way. The more healthy the family, the more freedom the different family members have to be themselves. The more dysfunctional the family, the more rigidly the family members are cast in roles from which they cannot escape.

Male-female relationships are the same. In functional relationships, both the man and the woman have a wide range of expression available to them. As the relationship becomes more dysfunctional, the range of behaviors that the relationship can withstand and still function becomes more narrow. The relationship becomes unsafe for a full range of feelings: certain topics must be avoided, certain feelings and desires become taboo, and repressed feelings can explode violently. The blaming begins. When the roles are cast in an unhealthy relationship, there is restriction and ever-increasing tension.

The solution to relationship problems is not to attack the person cast in the role of the "bad guy," any more than it is the solution to family problems to attack the member cast in the role of the rebel. The solution is to look at the system as a whole, to which all parties contribute and from which all parties benefit.

Codependency Systems

Men sometimes blame their emotional difficulties on the women in their lives. For example, they may blame their sexual frustration on the ways women dress. Women sometimes blame men for their frustration about not getting what they want in relationships, or for their economic or political difficulties. There seems to be little that men and women cannot blame on each other. Blaming others for the problems in our lives is the essence of *codependency.*

Building on the family roles work of Sharon Wegscheider-Cruse and others, therapists have developed a theory of codependency. This theory takes some of the basic ideas of family role therapy and applies them to individual romantic relationships.

Our penchant for black-or-white blaming makes it easy for us to believe that if we experience some misfortune at the hands of another, the other person or oppressing group never experiences similar pain. This is the "grass is greener" phenomenon: no matter which side of the fence we are on, the grass is greener on the other side. The other side has it better and easier than we poor victims have it.

For example, it is a common (but rarely spoken) tenet of feminism that only women experience oppression and limitation; men do not. Women experience fear; men do not. Women experience violent attack; men do not. Conversely, some men who find their shame, and share it in men's groups, believe that because they as men experience shame, women must not. People of both genders often think they have an exclusive charter on the pain of their oppression, and thus believe that their identified persecutors could never relate to or understand their pain.

"Grass is greener" people tend to polarize relationships into happy perpetrator (others) and miserable victim (themselves), rather than seeing their own power, their own choices, and the systems of their relationships.

This polarization is the hallmark of codependency. Codependent people resist seeing how their own actions affect what happens to them, and they have a genuine lack of perspective about how their perpetrator really thinks and feels. Said one such person, "As usual, I work and you play. I worry and you relax. I care and you don't. You feel good; I hurt."[37] The grass is greener on the other side.

In her ground-breaking book *Codependent No More*, Melody Beattie began the process of identifying codependency in all sorts of relationships, not just in alcoholic families. She gives a simple and elegant definition of codependency that we will explore and expand upon: "A codependent person is one who has let another person's behavior affect him or her, and who is obsessed with controlling that person's behavior."[38] Codependence is usually based on the belief that another person's behavior is causing all of our problems, and that if only we could control or stop that other person, all our problems would be solved. Because codependents are not able to see how their own behaviors and decisions help create the situations they are in, they feel powerless over their own lives.

Codependent people are often obsessed with blaming another person's behavior for their problems. "Codependents tend to become martyrs," Beattie says, "sacrificing their happiness and that of others for causes that don't require sacrifice,"[39] and blaming others for their problems. Codependents suffer from what author Judith Martin calls "the universal conviction that no one suffers more from the unjustness of life than oneself."[40]

Of course, there is a legitimate place for blaming. People who have truly been victimized when they really were helpless have every right to blame their victimizers, and this is a necessary stage of healing. But real victims, such as victims of child abuse, are different from people who have the power to change their situations, but either do not know they have this power or choose not to use it because of the benefits of staying in their relationship systems.

Ending Codependency

Beattie is quite clear about who is responsible for codependency: "It doesn't matter whose fault it is. Your codependency becomes your problem; solving your problems is your responsibility."[42]

In gender relationships, ending codependency requires less emphasis on blame and more attention on taking responsibility for our own lives and our own problems. Men can stop blaming their sexual frustration on the way women dress and act, and start changing their own behaviors to get more of what they really want. Women can stop blaming men for women's lack of committed relationships and women's economic difficulties, and start changing their behavior to get more of what they want. The first step in stopping codependent behavior is to understand it and identify it in your life. From there, it is simply a matter of exploring other, non-codependent, ways of behaving.

The Rescue Triangle

An example will help you identify codependent behavior. Susan and Jack have been married for three years. She is an industrial designer. He is unemployed, and looking for work. Susan complains that Jack mistreats her, usually when they are both tired. Let's listen in as they go out to dinner after a particularly difficult week.

Jack is staring quietly at his plate. It seems to Susan that something is bothering him, and she takes the initiative to make sure that he feels okay so they can have a good time. "Are you okay, honey?" she asks. "Is something bothering you?" With considerable coaxing, she finally gets him to talk about his day.

Jack tells Susan about an interview he had. It looks as if the work might be enjoyable but the job does not pay well enough to pay off his bills. "It seems like there's this trade-off in life," he says. "Either I get a job I hate that pays well, or do something that's not too bad but hardly make any money. I hate that, and there's nothing I can do. If I take this job, we won't be able to eat out anymore, or go to concerts. I won't be able to afford anything."

Susan tries to cheer Jack up. "You've just got to keep trying," she says. "There's got to be a job out there that you like and that pays well. Did you read that new job-hunting guide I got you? It looks like it has a lot of good ideas in it."

Jack's response is even more despondent. "It won't help. It's going to take a miracle for this to work out. It's like walking on eggshells at these interviews. If I say one wrong word, I could be kicked out on my ear. Anyway, employers don't like to see big gaps on people's resumes when they weren't working. If I don't get a job soon, no one will hire me because I've been out of work so long. My career could easily be over."

"Jack," Susan says, beginning to get exasperated, "Please don't get into that again. We're trying to have a nice dinner here. Don't you think you're being a little childish about this? Why don't you just get hold of yourself, and go for what you really want?"

"I don't know what you're being so self-righteous about," Jack counters. "You let your boss push you around whenever he wants to. You've got a lot of nerve telling me to go for what

I want, when you always put up with his manipulation. You're the one who's being naive and childish."

"I can't believe you're saying that!" says Susan. "It's my job that pays your bills while you fritter around out of work. If you weren't so helpless all the time, I wouldn't need to keep it at all! I only keep that job to pay off your bills, anyway! I can't believe you're treating me like this," she hisses, "I was just trying to help you feel better! You always do this to me!"

"Do what to you?" Jack retorts. "You started it. I was just having dinner, and you started being a bitch!"

Rescue Triangle Roles

To Susan and her friends, this interaction is simple to analyze. Susan is the victim of Jack, who is perpetrating upon her the ruination of her life. She does all she can—in fact, she goes out of her way to help him and to hold the relationship together, and he thanks her by calling her a bitch. He is the problem; she is the victim.

However, if we want to understand this interaction in more psychologically sophisticated terms than problem and victim, we need to see this relationship as a system. We need to understand the Rescue Triangle[43], a common behavioral dynamic in male-female relationships.

The Rescue Triangle was first described by the proponents of transactional analysis. They noticed that people tend to play "games" with each other in relationships, and the Rescue Triangle is one of these games. The Rescue Triangle helps us see the codependent roles that both members of a relationship unconsciously choose. The Rescue Triangle has three roles: Rescuer, Persecutor, and Victim.

Rescuing

Rescuing (also called caretaking) is a destructive form of helping. Help is destructive whenever the person "helped" does not grow or heal. A rescuer intervenes with the intention of preventing the person being rescued from experiencing the pain that would bring growth. Susan rescues Jack by trying to stop his pain. As long as the rescued person is kept from feeling the consequences of his or her actions, he or she stays in the same behavior patterns and is prevented from growing. Rescuing teaches people who see themselves as helpless to continue to see themselves as helpless.

According to Claude Steiner, a pioneer of transactional analysis, the role of rescuer has a special mystique in our society. "We are encouraged to be selfless, generous, and cooperative with people even if they are deceitful, selfish, stingy, and uncooperative with us."[44] Women are mystified about the dangers of rescuing "because sex-role programming is designed so that women will be an unpaid work force which makes the lot of males easier to bear."[45] Men are equally mystified about the dangers of rescuing, so they continue to rescue women by risking their lives to protect women, or by giving up everything in divorce.

The emotional payoff of rescuing is the feeling of being one-up, at least temporarily. Rescuers get to take care of, i.e., control, other people. As a result, they inflate for a time into god-like figures, all-powerful and free from their own problems. Viewing someone else as "the problem" also leads to a sense of innocence in the rescuer. Taking care of someone else produces a sense of being good. However, as we saw with Jack and Susan, the rescuer ends up as the victim of the rescued. Rescuing is the first corner of the Rescue Triangle.

Persecuting

Persecutors attack, sometimes with exaggeration, sometimes with the truth, usually with shaming, but always manipulatively and angrily. Persecuting comes naturally in a culture such as ours in which anger is so consistently repressed. Anger is always looking for a way to come out, and righteous persecution is the perfect opportunity.

There is something in everybody that likes to be the persecutor. Whenever we allow ourselves to become completely absorbed in anger at someone else's behavior, we are momentarily released from the pain and imperfection of our own lives. We persecute when we let out some anger on some problem person. Rescuers inevitably turn into persecutors, because rescuing inevitably makes us angry. Jack's constant helplessness imposes on Susan, and she finally gets angry.

Besides creating persecution, which is painful enough by itself, the rescue/persecute dynamic trains victims to continue to be victims. Instead of learning to take care of himself or herself and to avoid victimizing situations, the victim learns to count on being continually rescued and to keep behaving in the same way. Because being rescued interferes with one's ability to learn to take care of oneself, and fosters unhealthy dependence on others, the rescued person becomes resentful of the rescuer, rather than thankful. The rescuer, on the other hand, becomes angry that the rescued person isn't appreciative enough, or doesn't change enough, or becomes angry about the very weakness that rescuing has fostered. For example, I used to suffer from chronic low blood sugar, and I got into states in which I needed to eat, but nothing appealed to me. My girlfriend became a rescuer, taking care of me when I was experiencing low blood sugar. As a result, I stayed a victim, never learning to deal with my problem, until one day she blew up in persecuting anger about my helplessness. "Take care of yourself!" she told me. "I'm not feeding you anymore!" I was crushed, and experienced what Steiner predicted: "Every Rescue-Victim transaction will eventually result in a Persecutor-Victim transaction."[46]

Victiming

Victiming is harder to define. Just as there are legitimate rescues—it is perfectly legitimate for a lifeguard to rescue a swimmer from drowning—there are legitimate victims. Victiming, however, means assuming the role of the victim to manipulate other people *when one is not actually powerless*. People who do this habitually might be called "narcissistic victims," because they are adept at twisting every event and situation into an experience of being victimized. People who were legitimate victims, especially as children, often use victiming as adults to control other people, when they are not really victims.

The payoffs of victiming are *innocence* and *entitlement*: the victimized person is above all responsibility and is owed something as restitution for being put through an unpleasant experience. Victiming creates a self-righteous moral high ground from which to make demands. Susan uses this "victim's entitlement" to attempt to control Jack when she says he abuses her.

Beattie says that dedicated victims live their lives "sighing and crying, claim inability, proclaim their dependence, announce their overall victimization, and successfully control through weakness....Sometimes the weak are the most powerful manipulators and controllers. They have learned to tug at the guilt and pity strings of the world."[47]

Chronic victims have been taught that the only way they can have power without being "bad" is to have power covertly. The people who held overt, open power in their lives—most often their parents—too often misused that power to hurt them severely, so they have sworn off overt power forever. Instead, they prefer to manipulate from the background, using pathos, guilt-tripping, helplessness, and shaming. They create their own innocence by being victims of their boyfriends, their girlfriends, their parents, the government, the patriarchy, or the world.

They refuse to take responsibility for their own lives and for their own power in their lives.

Of course, controlling through victiming has its drawbacks, too. It is not pleasant. Victims are rarely happy, although their lives are often amazingly dramatic. "As victims," Beattie says, "we attract perpetrators."[48]

Susan and Jack

Susan and Jack's interaction illustrates all three roles in the Rescue Triangle. The first step is deciding who is powerful and who is powerless. Before the Rescue Triangle game can proceed, the players must decide who is the rescuer and who is to be rescued. Susan takes on the role of the rescuer, and Jack the role of the rescued. Susan's caring becomes rescuing when she decides that it is her responsibility to solve Jack's problems, whether or not he wants her to. She becomes a rescuer when she judges that Jack can't take care of himself, and that she has to do it. Like all rescuers, Susan trains Jack to continue in the behavior from which she is rescuing him. By showing him that she can and will solve his problems, she trains him to be someone who has problems and who brings them to her.

Through her rescues, Susan reinforces the very behavior in Jack which she hates. "We often accidentally reinforce the behavior we wish would extinguish," says trainer and author Karen Pryor. "We forget, or do not understand, that eventual reinforcement—that is, *any* reinforcement, good or bad— maintains the behavior."[49] Susan accidentally reinforces Jack's helplessness by supporting it with her rescues. This is a common dynamic in relationships, so it is essential to understand the concept of reinforcement. When a woman, for instance, is crabby, touchy, and mean to her lover, and he rushes to assure her that he loves her and everything is okay, he is reinforcing crabby, touchy, mean behavior. Pryor suggests that "a cheerful demeanor—no hand-wringing and upset—can do a lot to eliminate the usefulness of any display of moodiness or temper."[50] For Susan, not upsetting her life to take care of Jack when he appears to be unhappy would make his helpless behavior less attractive to him.

Jack responds to Susan's rescue offer by getting into his helplessness, and deciding that Susan is the powerful one who can save him. Susan's pleasure at being the powerful rescuer wears off as she becomes aware of the responsibility it entails. Although it feels good to be considered powerful, she starts to see Jack's weakness with the same contempt she feels for weakness in herself. She gets disgusted with him for being such a wimp, and decides he is needy for having accepted the help she offered. Now that Jack needs her help and really wants her support, she decides that he is imposing on her. She becomes angry at him for needing the very help she showed him she could give. She persecutes him for being weak by telling him he is being childish, and that he ought to get hold of himself. Jack, surprised by this attack when he is most vulnerable, becomes the victim.

When Jack gets angry about Susan telling him to grow up and starts attacking her in return, Susan completes the transformation from rescuer to victim. "After all I've done for him," she later says to a friend, "this is the thanks I get! It's always been like this. Men are always doing this to me. It's the story of my life. Where are all the good men?" Susan may receive pity from the people around her for days to come. As a victiming martyr, she can attempt to use shame about how Jack mistreats her to make him feel bad about himself and, at least temporarily, to control his behavior. However, Susan is completely unable to see her own part in perpetuating her situation. She, and most of our society, says that Jack is the problem. Not only is this unfair to Jack, it does not really help Susan. Instead of identifying and changing the dynamics of the relationship, this kind of useless blaming actually makes men's and women's problems worse.

The Rescue Triangle functions in steps. The rescuer's first step is deciding that the other person is helpless, and therefore must be rescued. The rescuer's second step is becoming angry about the rescued person's helplessness, and to attack. The rescuer's third step is becoming a victim, either of the rescued person's angry response, or of the constant imposition of the rescued person's neediness.

The rescued person's first step is to decide that the rescuer is powerful, and can actually rescue him or her. The rescued person's second step is to exhibit helplessness until the rescuer becomes the persecutor and attacks. The rescued person's third step is to become a victim of that attack, which leads to the fourth step, becoming angry and persecuting back.

Because the Rescue Triangle dynamic is so subtly ingrained in male-female relationships, it is worthwhile to look at more examples of it. Peter meets Sarah when he is teaching a class at a night school. She is intently interested in everything he says, and takes the lessons of the class to heart. She makes overtures of friendship, obsequiously soliciting advice from him on a number of topics. She loves his wisdom. She decides that Peter has all the answers, that he is powerful while she is powerless. The Rescue Triangle has begun.

Peter is seduced by her need, and by the affirmation he receives from her attention. He likes the way she hangs on his every word, and how she comes to him with her problems. He is there with help and advice whenever she needs it. He accepts that she is powerless, and he is powerful. He becomes the rescuer.

But Peter quickly becomes angry with Sarah's relentless helplessness, which he had previously rewarded with his attention. Now she seems weak and demanding, and he grows to fear her visits and her calls. He starts to think of her as a whiner, who is incapable of taking his marvelous advice. Dispensing his wisdom to her seems to him like casting pearls before swine. He becomes increasingly short-tempered, losing patience with her and her constant problems. He becomes the persecutor, disgusted by the very weakness he originally supported in her, and angered by her requests for the very help he demonstrated he would give. "I don't mind being a friend," he complains, "but she's imposing on me!" He asks her, "Why don't you just grow up?"

Throughout this dynamic, Sarah has believed that she is helpless and Peter is smart. As Peter goes from being a rescuer to being a persecutor, she becomes a victim. In time, she becomes a persecutor herself, telling him "I can't believe how you have betrayed me! What did I do to deserve this treatment? I thought you were there for me! I thought you were my friend!" The final result is two persecuting victims: Sarah is angry at Peter's persecution, and Peter is angry both at Sarah's demanding neediness and at her accusations of betrayal.

People can go through the dynamics of the Rescue Triangle with very little help from others. Maria is going to visit Steven, a possible romantic partner in another city. She's known Steven as a friend for over a year, but during their phone conversations it has become clear that an attraction is developing between them. He has asked her to visit so they can see what happens when they are together.

Maria believes that Steven expects her to be funny, charming, strong, and sexy on her visit. By taking it upon herself to be all of these things for him, she rescues him. Yet she finds herself resenting him almost immediately. "How dare he make these demands!" she thinks. "This whole visit is such a crock! I can't believe how he is pressuring me!"

Maria finds herself in this sequence: She decides Steven needs or expects something, and she believes it is her responsibility to provide what she thinks he expects. This is her rescue. Immediately she feels angry, deciding that he is imposing on her and pressuring her with his expectations. This is her motivation for becoming a persecutor. When she angrily calls Steven and tells him she does not want to visit because of how he is treating her, he may become a victim himself, be angry at the persecution, or he may simply be mystified. Sadly, Maria does not see that she is running the Rescue Triangle all by herself, driven by her unsupported assumptions about Steven, with little help from anyone else.

Richard and Cathy have been in a relationship for several years. Richard is often in emotional crisis, and needs Cathy to rescue and take care of him. Although Cathy has asked him many times to see a therapist, he refuses. Cathy continues to rescue him, dropping whatever she is doing to be with him in his need. In this way she teaches him that she will reward his crises with attention. He continues to need her.

Eventually Cathy concludes that Richard is using her. In her anger, she becomes the persecutor. They fight, and she snaps, "You always expect me to take care of you! I have a life, you know! You can't always expect me to be there for you!" Hurt by her attack, Richard has an emotional crisis right then and there. If that fails to draw Cathy back into the rescuer role, he becomes a persecutor, attacking her for her lack of compassion for his pain. Once again, the two partners become two persecuting victims, fighting over who is to blame for the fight over who is to blame. Sadly, this is an all-to-common scenario.

A Different Approach: Self-Empowerment
The Team Handbook, a quality improvement guide developed for use in business organizations, says that realizing most

problems are system problems "should discourage the common instinct to assign blame to individuals, and replace it with a desire to improve the system."[51] So, having that desire, what can we do to improve our relationship systems?

For each of the rescuers in our examples, there is an alternative to ending up as a persecuted victim. In the first example Susan, for instance, can recognize that Jack's sullen helplessness is not her problem, and she can decide to take care of herself the next time he becomes helpless. Let's look at how differently Susan and Jack's scenario might have gone if Susan were to refuse to rescue: When Jack appeared to be unhappy, she could remind herself that his moods are not her responsibility. When she asked him how he was feeling, and he said little in return, she could let it go at that, instead of coaxing his helplessness out of him. If she thought Jack expected her to provide solutions, she could either simply refuse to provide them, or she could ask him if that was really what he expected. She could also stop paying his bills if she decided this reinforces his helplessness. By refusing to rescue, she could have avoided getting caught in the Rescue Triangle. One way or another, Susan and Jack's relationship would have changed.

Peter could notice that he is rescuing Sarah by solving her problems, and he could decide not to get sucked into fulfilling her neediness. Maria could check out her assumptions about her visit with Steven, and if he really does expect things of her she does not want to give, she could choose not to give them. Finally, Cathy could take care of herself instead of taking care of Richard's emotional crises, and could refuse to take the role of therapist with him. Instead of reinforcing his helplessness and reliance on her, she could empower him to take some responsibility for his life, and to get professional help.

These are examples of *self-empowerment*, which is very different from rescuing or victiming. We can choose self-empowerment over playing the rescue/victim game. Such a route can be scary, though. When Susan empowers herself, she not only does what needs to be done; she takes the risk that her relationship with Jack might come apart. Furthermore, she also takes the risk that Jack might change his behavior and become powerful in ways she may not expect or like. When Cathy self-empowers, she risks that Richard might be alone in crisis, or that he might not love her anymore.

Self-empowerment is a path toward growth, choice, and gaining control over one's life. It means accepting that your actions have an effect on what happens to you. It is a lesson that both men and women do well to learn.

Learned Helplessness

In our first example, Susan decided to reinforce Jack's helplessness, rather than take care of herself. Why would she choose to continue to accept Jack's behavior? Why would she choose to accept his continual helplessness, which leads to her victimization, rather than using the power she has to get what she wants? In our last example, why would Cathy continue to allow Richard to use her as a 24-hour crisis counseling center? Why would she continue to tolerate, and even encourage behavior that hurts her so much?

People often believe that they have to put up with behavior they don't like from the people around them. This is because when we were very young, we *did* have to put up with the behavior of our family. The experience of having no control over what happens in our lives as children leads to what psychologist Martin Seligman calls *learned helplessness*. "Learned helplessness is the giving-up reaction, the quitting response that follows from the belief that whatever you do doesn't matter."[52] Dr. Seligman put people in situations in which they repeatedly and consistently had no power to affect or control what happened to them—such as receiving an electric shock or hearing an unpleasant noise. When he later put the same people in situations in which they *did* have control, he found that *they would not use it*. People stared uncomprehendingly at simple anagrams, without even trying to figure them out. They made no effort to stop unpleasant noises, although they could have done so with a simple movement, if they would only try. They had learned to be helpless, and that nothing they did mattered.

Chronic victims could try many self-empowering paths, but they do not, because they have learned helplessness. Many rescuer/victims, who continually support behavior that hurts them, are actually victims of learned helplessness. Having learned early in life that nothing they do affects what happens to them, they simply cannot conceive that life could be better for them. They rescue and try to shield others from the effects of their own behaviors. They act as victims to control others and to try to minimize the trouble in their "situations." They never dream that life could be fundamentally different for them.

Victims blame others for the problems in their relationships. Having learned helplessness, they are unable to make the fundamental changes necessary to really improve their lives. Even when they have power, they prefer to remain victims, and refuse to follow a self-empowering path. Even though being a victim is unpleasant, and does not get us what we want, at least it is familiar. It is often less frightening than the prospect of self-empowerment, which carries the risk of being alone.

Susan may have learned as a child to believe that she is helpless. As a result, with Jack, she is not able to see the power she has or how she could empower herself to get what she really wants. But—here comes the important part—*that is not Jack's fault*. Susan's inability to see her own power and how she maintains her victimization is *not* an example of Jack abusing her. A woman's staying in the victim role does not automatically mean that the man in her life is victimizing her, any more than a man staying in the ashamed role automatically means that the woman in his life is shaming him. They are both simply stuck in roles that they probably learned early in life and do not know how to get out of. Reflexively, they blame each other. This makes the woman feel more like a victim (angry and powerless), and makes the man feel more ashamed.

According to Steiner, "Oppression which involves some self-perpetuation or which is the result of lack of struggle against it"[53] is victiming. When you contribute to your one-down position, you are victiming. If your father abused you, and you find a boyfriend like your father and he abuses you, are your problems really your boyfriend's fault? If your mother and sisters shamed you, and you choose to be with a girlfriend who shames you in the same way, how effective is it to blame your girlfriend for all your problems?

Plenty of men and women are in genuinely abusive situations and relationships from which they cannot escape. But there are many more in situations and relationships which they could change, had they not learned to be helpless. These people experience real tragedy: they could change their lives to get more of what they want, but they are too demoralized to take the necessary risks.

These self-defined helpless people are inaccurate when they blame and condemn other people for all the pain and victimization they experience. If Susan rescues Jack, supports his behavior that hurts her, takes the rescuer/victim role for the payoffs of innocence and entitlement, and does not take the self-empowering path because she cannot see it, it is not Jack's fault. She is not victimized by Jack. She is victimized by her own help-lessness. And she will never change her situation by codependently blaming Jack for all of her problems. Society does her, as well as Jack, a great disservice by joining in his condemnation.

Escaping the Rescue Triangle

Much of the fighting that men and women blame each other for is in fact the fault of the Rescue Triangle dynamic. One side tries to rescue the other or asks for a rescue from the other, the rescue does not work, both sides get angry, and conflict erupts. Both sides look for resolution by trying to figure out who is to blame, which only fans the fire of conflict. Men and women need to understand the dynamics that govern the problems in their relationships.

Relationship difficulties are much easier to identify when they start with something clearly identifiable as conflict, rather than with a rescue or with a cry for help. Because the beginning of the Rescue Triangle dynamic looks something like love or intimacy, with a compassionate offer of help or a vulnerable request for assistance, it is hard to see the first steps that lead to conflict and emotional stress. This difficulty in seeing the beginning of the Rescue Triangle is compounded by our upbringing. Many of us were taught that love means rescuing, solving, and being responsible for other people's problems. Others were taught that if someone really loves you, he or she will always be there for you, no matter what inconvenience it causes in their lives. Our socialization disguises Rescue Triangle dynamics as loving intimacy, which makes conflict between women and men inevitable and difficult to unravel.

Escaping from the Rescue Triangle requires that we understand the difference between rescuing and genuine helping. Just because we want to stop rescuing others does not necessarily mean that we no longer wish to help others, or that we no longer wish to receive help. How can we tell the difference between helping and rescuing?

There are several warning signs of rescuing. Most importantly I can ask myself, "Am I treating this person as if he or she is smart enough to take care of himself or herself? Or am

I treating this person as if he or she is incapable of taking care of his or her own life?" This helps me see what behavior I am reinforcing. If I believe that the person I am helping is not smart enough or powerful enough to manage his or her own life, I am rescuing. I am reinforcing that person's helplessness.

Secondly, I can ask myself, "Am I getting angry at this person I am trying to help?" There is something about the "stuckness" of the person we are rescuing that makes us angry. We get angry when we determine that the other person is not willing to stop being helpless. They seem to be permanently helpless, and that makes us mad. Temporary helplessness does not have such an effect. I can help temporarily helpless friends without rescuing them. They may not feel powerful at the moment, but they and I both know that their powerlessness is not permanent. When I help these friends I do not feel angry, because I am not rescuing them.

Thirdly, I can ask myself, "Do I believe it is my responsibility to solve this person's problem?" If I do, then I am about to commit a rescue. Freely given help does not feel the same as help given under "rescuer responsibility" stress. Similarly, I can learn to tell the difference between my requests for help and my requests to be rescued. I can ask myself, "Do I think that this person is all-powerful? Do I expect this person to take care of me and solve my problem? Do I think I am incapable of taking care of myself?" If I answer yes to these questions, I am asking to be rescued, and asking for trouble.

Like so many other problems between men and women, the Rescue Triangle dynamic starts when we project a paradox. In this case, we project the paradoxical extremes of powerful and powerless, deciding that one side of the relationship is powerful while the other side is powerless. This basic projection sets up the Rescue Triangle.

For the Rescue Triangle game to go on, both sides must

be willing to play. The triangle goes best when the "helpless" one projects power at the same time the "powerful" one projects helplessness. Sometimes people are all ready to play out the triangle; other times they need to be seduced with tempting offers of how wonderful they would be if they rescued this weakness, or with such an appealing offer of "help" that the intended rescued will ignore the hook in it.

The solution is to retrieve our projections of powerful and powerless, and to remember that we are all sometimes powerful and sometimes powerless. We stop rescuing when we treat people as though they are powerful, and we stop needing to be rescued when we stop treating others as all powerful problem-solvers. When we stop projecting the paradox of powerful and powerless, and see people as they are, we can escape the Rescue Triangle.

This is good news, because it means that women and men can learn to avoid destructive relationship dynamics. By understanding that relationships are systems and by understanding the Rescue Triangle, we can notice when we give or hear a call for rescue, and we can choose a more self-empowering path.

It is important for men and women to understand relationship systems, because the sooner we see that our relationship problems are neither black nor white, the sooner we will be able to stop the blaming and shaming that causes so much trouble for us all.

Because women are usually cast in the victim role in our society, and men are usually cast in the persecutor role, our culture tends to blame men for problems in male-female relationships. Our codependent, blame-oriented culture stereotypes men as the abusers in relationships, while stereotyping women as helpless victims. This solves nothing, because it does not address the system of male-female relationships.

Seeing male-female relationships as systems is admittedly more complicated than saying "Jack is the problem and is abusing poor helpless Susan." It is also a lot more humane, useful, and accurate. It transcends our arguments about which gender has the power. It empowers women to see themselves as powerful, instead of seeing themselves as relationship victims, and it avoids shaming men as the cause of all relationship woes. When we see relationships with both a female and a male perspective, we find that relationships are neither black nor white. They are complex shades of grey, and great flights into bright colors. Relationships, we find, are systems.

Chapter 5

Stereotypes

M EN and women have both been dehumanized by our culture's stereotypes about them. Over the past several decades, women have opened our society's eyes about the stereotypes they have experienced. As a result, there has been real progress toward ending stereotypes' dehumanization of women. Ideas such as "women are only good for one thing" are routinely challenged all over our society. Our legal system intervenes to protect women from having to endure stereotypes. Although the job is by no means finished, women have been successful in changing the way our society stereotypes them.

If we want to end the dehumanization of both sexes, however, we must understand stereotypes about both women *and men*. Currently, men are one of only a few groups whom it is still acceptable to stereotype, and to stereotype viciously. People correctly challenge as offensive lies such stereotyping statements as "Asians can't drive," "A woman's place is in the kitchen," or "Blacks are lazy and shiftless." Yet, stereotypes about men, such as "Men have all the power" and "All men want is sex," are still widely considered to be "just facts." There are few

87

other groups—notably lawyers, doctors, and smokers—whom our society approves of abusing as we do men. It is still "politically correct" to stereotype men. An ad for *Bodyslimmers* says "While you don't necessarily dress for men, it doesn't hurt...to see one drool like the pathetic dog he is."[54] The front of a greeting card proclaims "Men are scum!" The punch line inside reads "Sorry, I was feeling generous there for a moment." The television show *Men Behaving Badly* opens with scenes of men being slapped repeatedly by women, and openly declares that "men are dogs." Negative stereotypes of men are still acceptable.

Stereotyping dehumanizes men. As we will see, stereotypes tell men again and again, throughout their lives, that they have everything, they run everything, they have ruined everything, they are expendable, and they are uncaring brutes who use and hurt women. When we stereotype men, we limit their options of behavior. When we teach men they are brutes, they are more likely to act like brutes. When we teach men they hurt women, they are more likely to hurt women. Men's reactive behavior, in turn, contributes to the persistence of stereotypes about men.

The "manly" behaviors and sacrifices our society expects of men are painful. Always having to win, succeed, and achieve is not only difficult, it is impossible. Being "on call" to die to protect women or to go to war at the government's command is stressful. The only way that men can make the expected sacrifices for career, women, family, and country is by repressing their feelings completely, and becoming dehumanized.

Just a Fact, Ma'am

The "just a fact" mentality makes stereotypes about men virtually invisible, and the dehumanization of men an almost invisible process. If we cannot see how men are dehumanized

88

by stereotypes, we find ourselves thinking that "inhuman" is just the way men are.

Stereotypes are difficult to see when they are disguised as facts. Once several friends of mine and I were preparing to give a presentation on men's issues. A friend of ours had saved several years' worth of newspaper and magazine articles about men and men's issues, and we spent an afternoon sorting through four big boxes of clippings, looking for examples of stereotypes about men.

We discovered that the stereotyping of men is a slippery fish indeed. Learning to see the stereotyping of women had not prepared us to see the stereotyping of men. We found that most stereotypes about men were not stated directly. Instead of saying "Men have all the power, and women are powerless," articles might say "Women, in their continuing struggle to achieve some degree of equality with men…." Instead of saying "Men commit all the domestic violence and women are always victims," they only reported and discussed the violence that men do to women, implying by omission that domestic violence against men does not occur.

Shere Hite, author of *The Hite Report on Male Sexuality*, asks men, "If women ran things, would they be fair to men?"[55] Although unstated, it's "just a fact" to Ms. Hite that men run the planet. The idea that men run the planet is actually a stereotype about men. The title of the book, *Why Jenny Can't Lead: Understanding the Male Dominant System,* presupposes that men's domination of everything is an obvious fact.[56] We often tacitly assume that stereotypes about men are facts, especially when the stereotypes themselves are not stated. Their very vagueness makes identifying them a somewhat nebulous task.

I suspect that all stereotypes are hard to see at first, and are considered "just the facts" until people challenge them. Women who first challenged the stereotypes about them undoubtedly experienced condescension and mystification from some men, just as men in the men's movement now experience condescension and amusement from some women. Just as many people thought the women's suffrage movement silly and irrelevant, today men who challenge the stereotypes about them often find that people around them see them as silly and irrelevant as well.

Although society in general and the women's movement in particular have encouraged women to see themselves as victims and to identify and fight against the stereotypes that hurt them, men, as the "designated perpetrators" in our society, have no such right. This complicates men's quest to understand and stand up against the stereotypes that hurt them. Our society's predisposition towards seeing only male privilege and only female disadvantage also makes the task more difficult.

Finally, the task of learning to see the stereotypes about men as clearly as we see those about women is made more difficult by men's shame about complaining about any abuse they experience: they learn they must "just take it or you're not a real man!"

If we wish to re-humanize men, we must first raise our awareness of the stereotypes about men. If we believe, for example, that "men have all the power," we will keep believing any argument based on that "fact." If we believe that men have no feelings and are naturally bad at relationships, we will never look for understandable sources of men's relationship problems.

Men need to be able to identify the stereotypes that operate in their lives. Because of the life-long dehumanization most men experience, they often are not as good at recognizing and honoring their own pain and sacrifices as women have become at recognizing and honoring theirs. Until men understand how they are stereotyped, they will be unlikely to protest when people tell them they have no pain and experience no disadvantages.

In this chapter we will explore how the cultural, stereotypic sacrifices demanded of men rob them of their humanity—and we will chart some ways back to creating gender reconciliation through the re-humanization of men.

The Stereotypes

Many "facts" commonly accepted about men are actually dehumanizing stereotypes. Briefly, some of them are:

• All men are alike.
• Men deserve the abuse they experience because men commit the violence.
• It's a man's world.
• Women make 69¢ for each man's dollar.
• Men are expendable.

There are also others, such as "women are victims and men are perpetrators," "only men are violent," and "all men want is sex," which we will discuss in Chapters 6 and 7. Let's explore these stereotypes in detail.

"All Men Are Alike!"

The first "fact" about men that is "all men are alike." When people (usually women) say or imply that "all men are alike," they do not mean that all men are alike in their good qualities. They are unlikely to mean that "all men are alike in their willingness to sacrifice themselves to protect women," or "all men are alike in that they deal with their wounds as best they can." Instead, when people say "all men are alike," they mean that all men personify what is *worst* about human beings.

This is a very unfortunate and dehumanizing stereotype about men. It clumps all men together as a single "man-thing" that hurts women. All stereotypes rely on the belief in the sameness of the members of the stereotyped group, and this stereotype is especially painful because it makes *all* men the same as *some* men are at their worst. This stereotype encourages people to see all men through the filter of the worst of what human beings can be. Making all men alike (and bad) gives people permission to blame *any man* for the actions of other men, whether those actions are real or imagined, and whether those actions occurred recently or historically. The stereotype, "all men are alike," gives people permission to punish men, personally and individually, for the real or imagined crimes of other men. When men internalize this stereotype, they learn to see themselves as deserving of punishment for the actions of other men.

Some men who believe in this stereotype give themselves special credit for not being like "other men." Women, too, sometimes grant this dispensation. Years ago, more than one woman told me, "Men are assholes, but you're different." They were complementing me, I suppose, for not being like a man. Similarly, I heard a feminist speaker at a rally declared the men there "honorary women," exempting us from the blanket condemnation of "all men are alike" and saying that morally, we were no longer men. The perceived need for such exemptions is sad testimony to the pervasiveness of the stereotype that "all men are alike."

As we break down any of the stereotypes discussed later in this chapter, the power of the belief that "all men are alike" is also broken. Every time we see men as individuals, and with compassion, "all men are alike" fades. When men, as well as women, are seen as human and as individuals, this stereotype will be gone.

"Men Deserve the Abuse They Experience, Because Men Commit the Violence"
The belief that "all men are alike" contributes to the

stereotype that men deserve to be abused, because men are so violent. The United States Department of Justice reports that men are the targets of violent assault 1.6 times as often as women[57], dispelling the myth that it's safer out there for men than for women. Nevertheless, otherwise compassionate people often dismiss this violence against men by saying "Yes, but it's men who are doing the violence!"

This attitude says much about how people feel about men. In essence, this attitude comes down to the belief that *because it is mostly men who do the assaulting, other men deserve to be assaulted.* Because of the stereotype that men deserve the abuse they experience, our society sees violence against men as nothing more than male perpetrators abusing each other. Because men are perpetrators, they are only getting their just punishment when they are attacked. Therefore, violence against men is much less important than violence against women.

This stereotype relies on the belief that "all men are alike," and lumps them together as "the violent ones." When we see men as individuals and human, we see how illogical it is to assert that "because other men are violent, an attack against Fred Smith (or whoever) doesn't really matter."

The fallacy of this belief becomes even more clear when we bring it down to a personal level: Because I am a man, I deserve less compassion than a woman, and a crime against me should not be punished as severely as the same crime committed against a woman. This may sound silly, but it exactly describes the situation in American society today: Many lawmakers support legislation making crimes against women more severely punished, and thus more important than crimes against men. This drive to dismiss violence against men follows naturally from the stereotype that men deserve to be abused because men commit the violence.

Such stereotyping is not new. In 1763, Benjamin Franklin

wrote about a revenge massacre of local American Indians:"The only crime of these poor wretches seems to have been, that they had a reddish brown skin, and black hair; and some people of that sort, it seems, had murdered some of our relations. If it be right to kill men for such a reason, then, should any man, with a freckled face and red hair, kill a wife or child of mine, it would be right for me to revenge it, by killing all the freckled red-haired men, women and children I could afterwards anywhere meet with...."[58] People seem to enjoy punishing entire groups for the actions of a few, even though such punishment is entirely unjust and ineffective.

Today, it is no more valid to say that male victims of violence are irrelevant because men commit most of the violence than it is to say that female victims of infanticide are irrelevant because women commit most of the baby-killing. It is no more valid than saying that female victims of child abuse are irrelevant because women commit most of the child abuse.[59] All truly victimized persons deserve equal consideration, no matter what their race or sex.

Compassionate understanding humanizes men by showing that all men are *not* alike, and that men who are victimized by violence deserve the same protection and compassion as victimized women deserve. As more people become able to see men as individuals and not just as victimizers, this stereotype will lose its power.

"It's a Man's World"

The third stereotype on our list says that "it's a man's world." If you are a man, according to this stereotype, your life is easy. It implies that each man is systematically granted tremendous special privilege and a life of ease. This encourages people to dismiss men's pain, because no matter how great their suffering, men are still much better off than women. Men are not subject to human suffering, according to this stereotype. Only women are.

The belief that it's a man's world has been a real driving force for feminism. The prevailing view is that women were kept out of the workplace, required to stay at home, caring for the house and children, while men left in the morning, and went to what humorist Dave Barry describes as a place where they "never have to take anybody, for any reason, to the potty,"[60] and came back in the evening. While women were suffering at home, goes this line of thinking, men were out doing what they wanted to do, running the world, having fun, and getting paid for it. On the surface, men appeared to have all power. Instead of having numerous stressful, life-shortening responsibilities, it could appear that he never experienced any human restrictions. From the woman's perspective, it could seem that the world belonged to him. (The reality, however, is that a man supporting a wife, kids, house, car, and a load of debt has far less freedom to choose what he does than his house-bound wife might imagine.)

The idea that "it's a man's world" recently showed up on a "comical" stick-up note. At the bottom of the sheet was a drawing of a woman, looking miserable and holding a squalling baby, while a smiling man with a briefcase is putting on his hat and going out the door into a sunny day. The caption reads, "It *was* a man's world." The note encapsulates the image of men having everything, and women having nothing; of men having fun, while women suffer. People may believe this popular idea, but it bears little resemblance to the reality of men's lives.

Because of our society's black-or-white belief that if women suffer limitation, men must not, and because of our lack of a male perspective to balance the female, we have accepted the "fact" that life is easy for men, and that the "man's world" is a great party from which women are excluded. As Jungian psychologist Robert Johnson says, "Women often labor under the delusion that life is really pretty easy for men, at least when compared to their own lot, and have no idea what a complicated struggle is really involved."[61]

Men are socialized to resist acknowledging having human difficulties, to never complain, and to make it look easy. That socialization makes this stereotype harder to identify. Boys are taught to laugh at their sacrifices, and to "shake off" the pain—in short, they are taught to not be human. Women, aware only of their own oppression and never having been men, have concluded from their own frustration and from men's apparent ease that men have everything they lack. That is simply not true.

A friend gave me an example of our society's belief that "it's a man's world." Each evening when his father got home from work, his mother would say, "A man may work from sun to sun, but woman's work is never done." Apparently, she had little compassion for how hard he worked, the sacrifices he made to support his family, or the pressures he endured to support his wife and children. His life, according to her (who never had to live it), was much easier than her own.

Similarly, a recent study reported that women work much more than men do. However, it did not take into account the difficulty of the work, nor whether the workers desired or enjoyed their work. A woman who wants to have children more than anything else may work at home with those kids many hours each day, but is her work really identical to, say, construction work? In terms of difficulty, risks to life and limb, levels of enjoyment, satisfaction, and difficulty, are these types of work really the same? It is easy for our society to judge that all work is essentially the same because our society believes that men have everything, and that men's lives are much easier than women's.

At a seminar about gender relationships, I saw another

example of the belief that the man's world is an easy time. One of the seminar leaders talked about how growing up on a farm, where she "had to" wash dishes and do other indoor work, while her brother "got to" mow the lawn, drive the tractor, and do the outdoor work. Now, farm work is dangerous for kids. Next to mining, farming is the most dangerous of occupations. One out of every five fatal farm accident kills a child. Each year 300 or more farm children are killed in farming accidents.[62] Nonetheless, the speaker saw dangerous outdoor work as a privilege because she was aware only of the restrictions in her own life, and because of her belief that the men's world is one big party that women are kept out of. She was blinded by the stereotype that "it's a man's world."

Demands Without Perspective

Many of the demands that women have made since joining the workforce have been justified. But the belief that "it's a man's world" has fueled increasingly extravagant demands. Either women will reach the lofty level of privilege which they *imagine* that men enjoy, or the stereotype that "it's a man's world" will die. Until one of these occurs, some women on the job will continue to believe that men are still holding the "good stuff" back from women. Getting rid of the stereotype would help women accept the real limitations of "the man's world," and would help men and women work together better.

The problem with this stereotype is that it encourages women to not believe they have equality until they have everything they *imagine* men have. They will keep making demands of men in the name of "equality." Recently, for instance, a woman was passed over for the job of running *American Airline's* LaGuardia airport office. Her superiors found her "stubborn and uncooperative," and she lacked an engineering degree, so the job was given to a male engineer. She charged her employer with sex discrimination, and won seven million dollars.[63] Not knowing what the "man's world" is really like, she expected and demanded the kind of special treatment she thought men experience. Women will continue making similar exorbitant demands until men stop being ashamed of what they have allegedly done to women and start acknowledging their own sacrifice and pain.

Women's demands are fueled less by vicious intent than by ignorance of what men's lives are really like. At some point, men need to tell women that, contrary to what they may have been told, *not getting everything you want* is a big part of the man's world. Women need more feedback from men who can acknowledge their own sacrifice and pain. Because of men's shame and unwillingness to acknowledge their pain, little has happened to challenge the beliefs that if it's difficult, men are still holding something back, and that if it's not great, it's not what men have.

In this respect, women experience a problem that affects any oppressed group: it is hard to tell how much of one's oppression is due to being a member of one's group, and how much is simply the general difficulty everyone experiences in life. Because women have no experience at being men, and because men have not been able to be honest with women about the difficulty of their experiences, women are understandably unable to tell how much of their difficulty is in fact caused by male oppression. Without data on how much difficulty men experience, women judge the root cause of their oppression based on what they *imagine* men experience. As we have seen, this does not work well.

The power of this stereotype will diminish as men learn to notice attempts to shame them into giving more than is fair by the accusation that they are holding something back. Men need to trust their own decisions about what is fair, and to give up their shame about treating women in business the same way they treat other men. As men learn to acknowledge their own feelings, pain, and sacrifices in the workplace, they will be better able to stand up to the shaming economic demands some women make. Men who are able to acknowledge their own pain and sacrifice do not feel obligated to automatically give women everything these women believe men have.

Women have not experienced being men. It should come as no surprise that sometimes their beliefs about what men have are just not accurate. The stereotype that "it's a man's world" is beginning to fall apart as women learn what the "man's world" is really like. "Nobody has truthfully told women what's in store for them if they move up, what they stand to lose as well as gain," says *Making the Most of Your First Job*, a book written by and for women in the workplace. "A promotion usually entails a lot of hard work, added responsibilities. There are not too many people who sit around and collect big, fat paychecks and do very little." The authors continue to break up the stereotype with this warning about career advancement: "You won't have the advantages you had on your first job. Mistakes you'll make will be highly visible.... Your boss won't be there to cover for you as much, or won't want to. That pressure, along with your increased work load, can contribute to a lot of stress.... There'll be a lot of those zombie-like days ahead." This is the unpleasant side of the man's world that women need to accept.

The authors ask women to look realistically at the man's world: "How do you feel about losing part, if not all, of your social life?"[64] This reality-check asks women to accept what men have accepted for a long time, and goes a long way toward counteracting the stereotype that the so-called "man's world" is a life of privilege. As a female friend of mine acknowledges, "Women have been pretty naive about the stresses of the workplace."

"Women Make 69¢ For Each Man's Dollar"

One permutation of the stereotype that "it's a man's world" is the belief that all men have economic power over all women. This stereotype says that all men, individually and personally, are economically powerful over each and every woman. This stereotype most obviously and most often appears in the claim that "women make 69¢ for *each man's dollar.*" This claim is quite different from the assertion that women, taken as a group, make 69 percent of what men make *as a group* (and even this is statistically incorrect[65]). It is not true that *each and every man* makes 31 percent more money than *each and every* woman, but the belief that they do is rarely challenged.

Belief in the 69¢ claim leads to selective inattention: the economic problems of individual men are ignored in favor of the economic problems of individual women because, after all, men make 31 percent more than women do. This, in turn, continues the dehumanization of men. A few men in our society earn a lot of money, so our society has focused on helping economically challenged women, while ignoring the economic problems of individual men. For example, affirmative action discriminates against *individual* men because men as a group earn more money than women as a group. This creates resentment in men, which reinforces the sense of distance between men and women. I, for one, have never made 31 percent more than the women around me because of my gender, and I am tired of being guilt-tripped by the implication that I do. Regardless of whether affirmative action is necessary, we must note that it is based on and perpetuates the stereotype that all men are economically powerful over all women.

Dr. Roy Schenk, an author and long-time observer of gender issues, has this to say about economic power: "I don't know whether it is men or women who dominate that small group of people who own the wealth of this country and of the world. I figure most of us don't benefit regardless of who owns it."[66] The 69 percent argument says that all men benefit, individually, at the cost of all women, individually. It leaves women feeling angry and demanding restitution from men. It also leaves men feeling guilty and ashamed. This is yet another example of the "grass is greener" effect. Many women have experienced men—such as their fathers or husbands—having economic power over them, and have jumped from that experience to the conclusion that all men have economic power over all women. The cultural belief that all men have economic power over all women casts all men once again into the role of the perpetrators. It falsely tells each man that he has economic power, and that to be a good man he needs to give this power to women.

Women's increasing economic power, with its concomitant responsibility, and women's growing understanding of the realities of the "man's world," are helping to dispel this stereotype. As more women experience being economically powerful over their own lives, they feel less need to generalize that power into the hands of all men.

"Men Are Expendable"

In our society, men's lives are less important than women's lives. When a ship is sinking, who is last into the lifeboats? The rule is women and children first; men last, if there is still room. Other examples of men's expendability include:

• Our culture expects men to take risks and make sacrifices to protect or help women. In fact, being willing to unflinchingly risk is part of our society's definition of manhood. But have you ever heard of a woman taking a bullet to protect her husband? She may decide to, but she's not *expected* to, as men are. The brother of men's issues author Warren Farrell died in an avalanche when he went ahead to make sure the way was safe for his girlfriend.[67] The expectation that men will auto-matically do this kind of thing says that men's lives are less important than women's lives. As long as men unconsciously follow this societal expectation, they will be unable to *choose* the risks they take for women.

• If we considered men's lives to be as important as women's lives, we would debate as much about drafting young men for combat as we do about drafting and sending young women into combat. But because men's lives are not seen as equally important, we hardly discuss it at all. The Selective Service says, "If you are a female…you are not required to register [for the draft]. However, if you are a male 18 through 25 years old, you must contact Selective Service."[68] Failure to register leads to punitive measures against men which women never experience. Young men who refuse to sign up for the draft are denied college financial aid and government employment. A proposal to require only women to register for the draft would be met with outrage because we value women's lives over men's.

• If women died seven to ten years younger than men, American society would respond, because women's pain and women's agendas are important considerations to our culture. But because men's lives matter less than women's, men's pattern of early death is hardly acknowledged as a problem.

Of course, this is not simply a one-sided dynamic. There are also ways in which women are seen as expendable. But the idea that men are expendable is an especially difficult and destructive stereotype for men. It teaches men to ignore abuse to themselves in order to protect women, even at the cost of their own lives. It tells men to ignore their own feelings and their own pain, when it is convenient for society to have them do so. It makes men's lives much more expendable than anybody else's. This sense of expendability profoundly devalues and dehumanizes men. Seeing men as full-fledged human beings, whose lives are just as precious as women's, will end this stereotype.

Our culture will only regard men as fully human beings when men so regard themselves. The kind of deep emotional work that pervades much of the men's movement is a crucial step toward genuine self-esteem among men. No matter how we were taught to see ourselves as less than human, expendable protectors of women, we are responsible if we keep doing it once we know it diminishes us. Men's awakening to their true human worth will eventually destroy the stereotype that men are expendable.

"Men Don't Love Right"

The stereotype that "men don't love right" takes many forms: "Men don't share feelings right," "Men don't do relationships right," "Men don't nurture right," and "All men want is sex!" We examined this stereotype in depth in the chapter on shame, as it is one of the central shaming messages for men.

As we have seen, men are the socially-designated custodians of achieving, and women were long considered generally inept "on the job." Women have struggled hard to overcome this prejudice. At the same time, women are the designated custodians of relationships, an area in which men are still considered generally inept.

Of course, it is not surprising that men—in general—are not as expert at developing and maintaining relationships. Achievement in the public sphere has been men's major area of strength; feelings and relationships have been their main area of weakness. This has given rise to the stereotype that there is something inherent in men that cannot love right, and therefore that whatever a woman wants in a relationship is by definition best for the relationship. Many men have experienced women's efforts to keep them "in line" in relationships, which take a heavy toll on love and spontaneity.

The bulk of the relationship literature addresses one question: What is wrong with men that keeps them from giving women what women want? Variations on this question include "Why won't he open up?" "Why can't he commit?" "Is he a Peter Pan? A man-who-hates-women? A guy with cold feet?" However, there is no objective evidence that what women want in relationships is automatically what is best for both men and women. Conversely, there is no evidence that what men may want is inherently less healthy. It is true that large numbers of men have difficulty opening up, or committing to relationships in ways women might want, but that does not mean that something is necessarily wrong with the way men relate. Perhaps a man senses that a woman is less interested in him as a person than in what she can get from him (for example, commitment, economic security, or a father for her children). Perhaps his career is enough commitment for right now. Perhaps he has seen his male friends go through divorce, and does not want that to happen to him. Perhaps he has a wounded inner child who needs healing more than the responsibility of a committed relationship.

These are examples of human reasons why men do not always work at relationships in ways women want. Reasons and wounds make men relate the way they do, not some shameful essential defect, as implied by the stereotype "men don't do relationships right."

Who Will we Blame?

Men are stereotyped in our culture, and there are many good reasons to end that stereotyping. But what is at risk if we give up stereotyping men? How has it served our society to stereotype men, and what might we have to give up if we stop?

Most of the stereotypes we have examined allow us to

blame men for all the problems of the world. The notions that it's a man's world, all men are alike, and men deserve the violence they experience—all these allow women (and men) to point to men, as a group, as The Problem. Like all stereotypes, these stereotypes let us simplify our problems by giving us someone to blame for them. They allow us to complain about our lives and the state of our world, without taking responsibility for making any changes.

If we end negative stereotypes about men, whom will we blame? Doctors? Lawyers? Cigarette smokers? There are no plausible villains left. If we are to give up stereotyping men, we will also have to give up our collective desire to blame someone else for the state of our lives. If our culture gives up stereotyping men, we will have to stop defining ourselves as essentially helpless victims of some all-powerful abusers. We will have to be responsible for who we are, and for the state of our lives. Stopping blaming men requires us to stop blaming altogether.

Just as important, this will also require men to stop blaming women for stereotypes about men. Ending stereotypes will not come about by men blaming women and somehow getting women to change. Nor will it happen through women getting men to change. Men will have to make the changes they want in their own lives. It is up to men to say "No! I'm not going to follow that stereotype this time!" For any of us to get what we want in our lives, it is *we* who must change.

Although both men and women perpetuate stereotypes, men will disempower themselves if they wait for women to change first. It is great for men when women change their stereotyping behavior, just as it is great for women when men change theirs. But as long as a man needs women to change before he can be happy, he will go through his life feeling helpless and blaming women.

Exploring gender issues can seem like an invitation to bring our past wounds unnecessarily into the present, and to blame people who are presently in our lives for the way someone of the other sex treated us long ago. However, a person of the other sex who acts in a stereotyping way is *not* our father who yelled at us, nor our ex-wife who convinced us we were shameful, nor any of the other people of that sex who have hurt us. People acting in a stereotyping way are nothing more than people acting in a stereotyping way, and it is counter-productive to attack them with the full brunt of our rage and pain. People who stereotype men may need to be set straight, but for most of us, the people in our lives right now are not the same people who wounded us.

Women have exploded many stereotypes about them ("Women are irrational," "Women are just 'dumb broads,'" etc.). Now it is men's turn to do the same. When people start seeing how negative stereotypes operate in men's lives, and start acknowledging the difficulties men have experienced and the sacrifices they have made, stereotypes about men will fade away.

As men become aware of the ways they are stereotyped, they can heal, but they also risk falling into blaming, and getting stuck in eternal recitations of the injustices against them. Most people have met women who are stuck in lamenting how women in general, and they in particular, have been victimized and hurt. Such women blame *all men*, and bring their past hurts into every situation. There are also men who blame women for all their problems, and for the problems of the world. No matter who does it, blaming is unattractive. As we give up the blaming stereotypes about men, we can give up blaming altogether. Angry women may still attempt to shame and emotionally repress men who challenge stereotypes, but the situation is improving. Some angry women still do not want to give up the benefit they receive from stereotypes about men—

having weak, ashamed, and easily manipulated men around who are willing to sacrifice themselves for women. In increasing numbers, however, women are getting past their anger at men and are becoming interested in truly equal relationships. A man who challenges stereotypes about men is more likely than ever before to experience support from the men and women around him.

By identifying stereotypes about men, we can consciously minimize their effects in our lives. We can re-humanize men, see both men and women as fully human, and thus help end the war between the sexes.

Beyond the Blame Game

Chapter 6

Violence

L INGUIST and social critic Noam Chomsky once observed that, "People, on the whole, tend to behave like people." Simple though it may sound, this is the basis of a fair and equitable view of men and women. At their best, men and women tend to behave like people at their best. At their worst, men and women tend to behave like people at their worst. Strangely, many people resist the idea that women, at their worst, behave the same as men at their worst.

This chapter will explore how we are all in fact human. Each of us, regardless of our gender, has the whole cycle of violence, and the potential to be both victim and perpetrator, within us. We will see how people tend to behave like people, and that neither gender is better or worse than the other.

"Women Are Victims, Men Are Perpetrators"

Our society's belief that women are victims and men are perpetrators has made violence against men all but invisible. The "fact" that men are always the abusers has directed our society's attention exclusively toward violence against women. Preventive measures against violence are far more often directed at protecting women than at protecting women and men. Women's ride services, battered women's shelters, and domestic abuse consciousness-raising events are all essential, and just begin to address the problem of violence against women. The point is that there is *nothing* comparable for men. The existence of such services only for women gives the impression that no similar services are needed for men. As we will see, there is ample evidence that they are.

The stereotype that only men commit domestic violence implies, to the public mind, that men can never be victims. Our society believes that men, as perpetrators, cannot experience domestic violence. The phenomenon of battered men remains a well-kept secret because of the belief that women are the only victims. In researching this book, I have seen more media coverage of battered lesbians[69] than of men who are battered by the women in their lives.

Selective Inattention

Cultural denial of certain behaviors is not a new phenomenon. It has taken many decades to break through our culture's denial of domestic violence, even to the present extent. Each type of abuse, when first "discovered," has been vigorously denied by most of our society. Over time, each type of domestic abuse has become recognized as a real problem.

For instance, in the late nineteenth century, Sigmund Freud noticed that a number of his clients recounted tales of child-hood sexual abuse. When he published his findings, the resulting controversy forced him to recant. He "reformulated" his theories to say that adults didn't *really* sexually abuse children; these were merely delusional fantasies made up by his clients. In 1897, the people of Vienna were simply not able to accept that parents, at their worst, could behave so badly. Only recently has our society begun to accept the truth about sexual abuse.[70]

For a long time, physical child abuse was also screened out by our culture's selective inattention. A pediatrician in the 1950s assured us that no adult would ever beat a child. He claimed that if child abuse ever happened at all, it was only an isolated incident. If parents could damage their children, he argued, the survival of humanity would be in danger. Natural selection would surely put an end to such abusive behavior.

People's emotional issues about how parents behave made it imperative that they stay in denial about child abuse. Our culture was simply not ready to accept that parents could behave so destructively toward their children. That was the 1950s. Decades later, child abuse is at last being openly discussed. Now we know that there has long been, and still is, a phenomenal amount of child abuse.

We see the same pattern of denial and gradual admission in wife battering. 1974, researchers Maccoby and Jacklin concluded that "there can be little doubt that direct force is rare in most modern marriages. Male behavior such as that...would be considered pathological...and if widespread would endanger a species."[71] In the 1970s, people's emotionally charged beliefs about how men behave kept them in denial about men's domestic violence against women. Now, thanks largely to feminism, we are aware of the incredible amount of wife abuse in our culture. Despite the evidence, only in recent years have many people come to accept that some men treat their wives violently.

There is now extensive evidence that, at least in the home, men and women resort to violence a surprisingly similar amount. They hit each other with nearly the same frequency, for the same reasons, and with the same injurious intent. The recent "discovery" that some men are physically abused by women is still so controversial that, according to domestic violence researchers Murray Straus and Richard Gelles, most social scientists "have given the topic of battered men a wide berth."[72] Our emotionally-charged beliefs about how men and women behave keep us in denial about women's physical abuse of men. In spite of the evidence, many people still cannot accept that women can be violent to men.

Despite researchers giving this topic a "wide berth," there is a growing and impressive body of evidence that men and women both behave like people. A certain percentage of people—of either gender—become violent when they are angry, exasperated, or at their wit's end. For example:

• Researcher Susan Steinmetz found that 39 percent of husbands and 37 percent of wives had thrown things at each other; 20 percent of both husbands and wives had struck their spouses with their hands; and 10 percent of both husbands and wives had used hard objects to strike their spouses. Her data show that men and women tend to be equally violent.[73]

• Murray Straus and Richard Gelles, two of the leading researchers of domestic violence, found that 12.1 percent of husbands and 11.3 percent of wives were victims of spousal violence. They observe that "in marked contrast to the behavior of women outside the home, women are about as violent in the family as men." [74]

• In another article, Murray Straus estimated that 1.8 million women are domestically abused each year in the United States. He also estimated that there are 2.1 million domestically abused men.[75]

• Nisnonoff and Bitman found that 18.6 percent of men and 12.7 percent of women reported being struck by a spouse. They concluded that "men often are the victims of spousal violence."[76]

• Merlin Brinkerhoff and Eugen Lupri found that 2.1 percent of men in "couple" relationships had kicked, bit or hit their partners with a fist in the last year, while 3.7 percent of

Violence

women in those relationships had done the same. They also found that 10.8 percent of women and 6.8 percent of the men had, in the previous year, "threatened to hit or throw something at the other."[77]

• In a study of violence in dating relationships, David Sugarman and Gerald Hotaling found that 33 percent of men commit a violent act, compared with 39 percent of women.[78]

• Battered women can be violent, too. Jean Giles-Sims found that 50 percent of women in domestic abuse shelters had assaulted their partners in the previous year. Disturbingly, she also found that 42 percent would assault their partners within six months after leaving a shelter.[79]

• Researcher Coramae Mann found that women who kill their spouses often have a prior habit of resorting to violence. Of women who kill their partners, 78 percent have prior criminal histories, and 55 percent have histories of violence.[80]

• According to the U.S. Department of Justice, "in spouse murders, women represent 41 percent of killers. In murders of their offspring, women predominated, accounting for 55 percent of killers. When a mother killed her own child, she was almost twice as likely to kill a son than a daughter. But when a father killed his own child, the offspring he killed was about as likely to be a daughter as a son."[81]

Clearly, domestic violence is not a black-or-white issue. Many other studies—almost all the studies that are not based on self-selecting samples or police reports—show the same trend. In fact, one survey of research on aggression found that 61 percent of studies showed that men are no more aggressive than women. [82] The evidence is unmistakable that men and women can become abusive under certain circumstances. Men are not inherently more violent than women. Women are not naturally more peaceful than men. For better and for worse, people tend to behave like people.

Like most readers, I was initially surprised by these statistics. As I examined the research and my reaction to it, I found that my surprise came from my own sexist expectation that women, given the same opportunities and situations as men, would behave better than men. My encultured belief in men as perpetrators and women as victims made me want to deny the evidence that women can be as violent as men.

Research indicates that people hit "because they can." The privacy of the home, according to Murray Straus, enables both men and women to treat "the marriage license as a hitting license."[84] Men, as is well known, have been able to hit women because men are often physically larger. But what about the other side? What gives women the message that it is all right to hit men?

Women are able to abuse their mates because men are even less likely than women to complain. While there has been a tremendous and long-overdue effort to educate women to recognize and report their victimization, the almost complete denial of women's violence toward men has driven battered men even further into isolation and loneliness. Combined with men's shame and belief that they, as oppressors, probably deserve whatever women do to them, and the fact that battered men have nowhere to go, it is easy to see how violence against men is ignored. For example, one man told me, "I can testify for myself, as well as for two other gentlemen who went through physical abuse by their wives. The police just laughed at the complaint." Another man wrote, "Blood streamed down my face… Lacerations and multiple abrasions marked my back and groin. I told the officer that I wanted the crime report to note my injuries and the names of witnesses. He responded: "We ain't takin' a report from you, buddy." Another officer later told him, "You gotta be kidding, buddy. Women don't beat men."[85]

The sense of entitlement commonly felt by victims also

empowers women to be violent towards men. Over the past few decades, women have been taught that they are victims of men. Unfortunately, some women now feel entitled to "get men back." As one woman said to me, "After 4,000 years of women's oppression, any pain men experience seems pretty insignificant." After 4,000 years of oppression, this woman seemed willing to inflict some of that pain.

Yet another reason why violence against men is more acceptable than violence against women is the basic difference in our culture's perspectives on men's and women's violence. Violence done by men is likely to be interpreted as abuse, but violence done by women is often interpreted as self-defense or empowerment. People love to punish a perpetrator, whether real or imagined, so it seems that justice is done when women "get men back."

There are ominous signs that we live in a climate of increasing anger toward men. The Roper Organization surveyed 3,000 women using a word-for-word duplicate of a questionnaire used twenty years previously. The survey shows that women are increasingly angry and dissatisfied, and are aiming their anger and dissatisfaction at men. Fifty-eight percent of the women agreed that "most men think only their own opinions about the world are important," up 50 percent since 1970. Fifty-five percent of the women agreed that "most men find it necessary for their egos to keep women down," up from 49 percent 20 years ago. And 53 percent agreed that "most men are interested in their work and life outside the home and don't pay much attention to things going on at home," up significantly from 39 percent in 1970.[86] This anger fuels the sense that men deserve the violence they experience, and drives some women even farther from feeling compassion toward men.

Furthermore, the pressures on women to be "good," meaning virtuous and submissive, has created a backlog of anger and frustration that can come out violently in relationships. Women's rageful anger comes out where it can, just as men's does. According to Straus and Gelles, women perpetrate 62 percent of violence against children.[87] Furthermore, mothers kick, bite, punch, and threaten or use a gun or knife on their child more than half again as often as fathers.[88]

Ending the Denial

As Straus says, "The old cartoons of the wife chasing the husband with a rolling pin or throwing pots and pans are closer to reality than most—and especially those with feminist sympathies—realize."[89] Yet many people choose to remain in denial. What is the emotional imperative that makes it so hard for us to believe that women at their worst could possibly behave like men at their worst? Most people are initially skeptical of the statistics quoted above. That couldn't possibly be true, they say. Why would people choose to be skeptical about these numbers, when they have no trouble accepting statistics identifying men as the sole abusers?

There are two reasons why we might choose to be skeptical about domestic violence against men. First, it is not what we've always been told. It is not what we are used to hearing. These statistics, which have been largely suppressed, surprise us. The second important reason is that we need someone to blame. It's the blame game again—if we can't blame men, whom can we blame? It rarely occurs to us that we might not need to blame anyone. Because our society trains us to see everything adversarially, in terms of black and white, right and wrong, good and evil, winner and loser, we have a hard time accepting that people behave like people, and that it may not be anybody's fault.

The tendency of police to ignore violence against men, the education of women about their victimization, the socialization of men to never complain, men's shame about being men, victims' entitlement to "get men back," and the increasing anger of women—all these factors encourage us to stay in denial about women's violence toward men.

Emotional Abuse

Many women are well aware that verbal battering is a very real form of violence. In her book *The Battered Woman*, Lenore Walker says: "The slow emotional torture which produces invisible scars is as abusive as the quick, sharp physical blows."[90] A counselor at a women's center reports that "women in our support group always talk about psychological abuse as the worst. That's the part that is hidden; that's the slowest to heal."[91] In her book Toxic Parents, Dr. Susan Forward notes that "Insulting names, degrading comments, and belittling criticism can give extremely negative messages which can have dramatic effects." She quotes a caller to her radio show, who said, "If I had to choose between physical and verbal abuse, I'd take a beating anytime. You can see the marks, so at least people feel sorry for you. With the verbal stuff, it just makes you crazy. The wounds are invisible. Nobody cares. Real bruises heal a hell of a lot faster than insults."[92]

Emotional or verbal violence may be the most common form of violence that people do to each other, but there is almost no information about it. The "invisible beatings" that women and men inflict on each other deserve far more attention than they have received. Emotional abuse happens whenever people encourage, trick, or coerce others into feeling bad about themselves. If a man's lover continually picks at him about how he looks, behaves, thinks, and smells, he is being emotionally abused, and needs to know it. If a woman's boyfriend continually belittles her body, or her intelligence, she is being abused as well. Too often people do not even recognize emotional abuse. Men, who are punished for complaining about hardships, have an especially difficult time.

Abuse vs. Feedback

Learning to identify emotional abuse requires learning the difference between abuse and feedback. Sometimes it makes sense to take advice from other people. Sometimes the people close to us have accurate information about us and about our effects on others, which we benefit from hearing. But there is a vast difference between saying, for example, "I've noticed that whenever I say I want to talk about our relationship, you speak less and appear to become uncomfortable; when I see this, I feel angry," and "You don't really care about me! All you want me for is sex!"

Abusive statements often start with the word "you," or "you just," as in "You just think you can use me, and then walk away!" or "You're disgusting! You just think I'm stupid!" These statements center around the speaker's judgments about the listener, stated as facts. If you hear yourself beginning many sentences with "you," "you always," or "you just," there is a good chance you are about to be verbally abusive. If you are being told these things, it is likely you are being verbally abused.

Feedback statements, in contrast, are "I" statements. They center around the thoughts, feelings, and judgments of the speaker, not those of the listener. "I" statements convey the speaker's experience, without claiming that they are facts. For example, let's assume that a woman tells her boyfriend, "When I talk about my feelings and you don't say anything, I think that you don't care about me, and I think you only want me for sex. When I think that, I feel angry." In this example, she is owning her judgments and feelings as her own. She is not accusing him of not caring about her. She is saying, however, that when he does not talk, that is the judgment *she* makes. This kind of feedback is useful. Instead of labeling her partner as uncaring, sullen, lazy, or whatever, she says what she feels and thinks, *and checks out the accuracy of her conclusions.* She reflects that her partner is not talking, and she asks why. She gives him the information that when he doesn't talk, she thinks he doesn't care. This kind of communication is a lot more useful than "You don't care about me," which is nothing more than a conclusion about someone else's behavior, stated as a fact.

One powerful way to learn to recognize emotional abuse is to become aware of how and when *you* do it. Practicing "I" statements until they become natural will make you less abusive yourself, and will help you identify "you" statements when they are used against you. Being able to distinguish "I" statements from "you" statements allows you to distinguish feedback from abuse.

Examples of Emotional Abuse

We have seen that men have often used their achievement power to "set women right" on the job, working on a car, or getting something done. We have also seen that women often use their feeling power to "set men right" about how men should express their emotions and behave in relationships. This emotional abuse of men is as destructive as men's economic abuse of women has been.

I asked a number of men who have developed their emotional awareness whether they had ever experienced emotional abuse from women. Every man had. Here are a few of their examples of emotional violence.

One man told how he used to be so emotionally dependent on his girlfriend that he would take any amount of abuse to avoid losing her support. The abuse centered around her dissatisfaction with the way he loved her. "I can't tell you how to do it," she lamented, "you have to *want* to do it." In fact, he already wanted to, and felt terrible for not knowing how. She was telling him he was no good as a loving person, and he believed her.

Another man reported receiving a lot of "you are disgusting" abuse from an old girlfriend. "It was as if she thought men are basically disgusting but necessary, which is not an attractive attitude. I didn't dress right, I didn't smell right, I didn't do my hair right, my friends were gross—she was abusing me, but I felt like a loser! And my sexual fantasies, my pornography, really intimate private things about me, were disgusting, disgusting, disgusting." (It is sad to note how often angry women call men "disgusting." This is emotional abuse, just as calling women names is.)

Of course, name-calling, swearing, yelling, threatening and raging are equally abusive when women do it to men as when men do it to women. The women's movement has helped women to recognize emotional and verbal abuse against them. This is important, but has given the impression that only women suffer emotional abuse, and only women need to be helped. If women and men are to heal their relationships, both women *and men* must begin to identify and stop the physical and emotional abuse they give and receive.

What's at Stake

Abuse of men, both physical and verbal, occurs. It is a real problem. Unfortunately, the stereotype that to be a real victim one must first be female keeps battered men from receiving the kind of help and support that we are belatedly offering to battered women. There is no place for battered men to go because the stereotype prevents the problem from being officially acknowledged.

The convergence of the women's and men's movements present a unique opportunity to stop projecting the role of "violent perpetrator" onto men and the role of "peaceful victim" onto women. As Noam Chomsky reminds us, people tend to behave like people. This is the belief that goes beyond blame, and is the belief of the future. We can give up looking for a victim to save and a perpetrator to hate. We are both more alike, and more variable in our behaviors, than we have been lead to believe.

As we acknowledge domestic violence against men, what is really at stake is the belief that women are exempt from unpleasant behaviors. In other words, what is at stake is the belief that women are inherently more moral than men. But as the research shows, feminists are right: anything a man can do, a woman can do. The new twist on this old feminist slogan is in the realization that men and women can do the same things when they are at their worst, as well as when they are at their best.

Someday, society's denial of women's domestic violence toward men will seem as strange as society's former denial that children and women are abused. By developing our perspective on inter-gender violence, we can bring that day closer.

Chapter 7

Sex

TED and Donna have been in a steady sexual relationship for almost four months, and they enjoy each other's company very much. One night Donna begins to talk with Ted about making commitments to each other, but he stops her. "Please!" he says. "I like you, but do we have to get into heavy commitment? Why can't we just keep going the way we have been, and see what happens?" This does not please Donna. She is more concerned about Ted's emotional availability and his commitment to their romantic relationship than about their sexual connection.

Meanwhile, Martin and Cynthia are on their third date. They are on her living room couch, kissing with increasing passion. Martin moves to unbutton Cynthia's blouse, but she stops him. "Please!" she says. "I like you, but does it have to be sexual? I want something more. Let's stop and just hold each other." This does not please Martin. He is more concerned about her sexual availability and her commitment to their erotic relationship, than about their non-sexual emotional connection.

The men and women in these two examples seem totally

different. She's into feelings, he's into sex. She wants romance, he wants lust. For some, men's and women's different approaches to sex are the final proof that men and women are irreconcilably different, and that women and men are truly aliens to one another. In fact, however, romantic desire and sexual desire are different sides of the same coin. It's the by-now-familiar paradox, and this time it centers on sex.

Paradox and Sexuality

These two examples show how men's and women's experiences of sexuality are often sharply paradoxical. We tend to reconcile paradoxes by aligning ourselves with one pole and taking a stand against the other. In this way, we satisfy our desire to be consistent, and reduce the "cognitive dissonance" of holding contradictory points of view at the same time. We make one side of a paradox wrong, and the other side right.

Romance and sex are a paradox of the human psyche. They coexist in each of us, but they often seem to be in conflict, and to be as different as any two drives can be. Romance and sexuality live on opposite sides of a paradox. Because romance and sex are opposite sides of the same paradox, they have more in common than we often thinzk. While romance is an emotional fantasy, sexual desire is a physical fantasy. Romance is the emotional form of love, and sexual desire is the physical form of love.

The idea that our sexual desires are a form of love is hard for many people to accept. Sexual desire has a bad reputation. People often approach sexual desires with disdain, considering such desires to be using, uncaring, "just fulfilling animal desires," and so on. Sexual desire is bad! It is difficult to talk about sexual desire without the powerful emotional charge of these negative associations.

Thinking of sexual desire as a form of love, on the other

hand, removes the judgments. Sexual love is neither good nor bad; it just is, so we can think about it dispassionately. It is not "bad" just because it is not committed. It is not "bad" just because it doesn't want to know you intellectually. Instead, it wants to know you sexually. Sexual love has a place in intimate relationships, just as emotional and intellectual love have their places. When it gets out of balance with other forms of love, people get hurt, in the same way that emotional love can turn into enmeshment and intellectual love can turn into mind games.

When the negative connotations about sexual desire are removed, we can see that men and women have different experiences with sexual love and attention. Women often receive sexual love and not much else. Men, for reasons we will examine in a moment, are often interested in loving women sexually and can ignore their other qualities. Consequently, women develop a tremendous need to be loved in non-sexual ways. Receiving sexual love from men to the exclusion of all else has led women to see sexual love as inconsequential or valueless. This surplus of sexual love can make men's sexual love of women seem scary and insulting. Women are understandably sick of being force-fed too much sexual attention.

Men, on the other hand, have an entirely different experience. Instead of experiencing an outpouring of sexual love and desire from women, men learn that they must perform outstandingly to even earn the opportunity to give sexual attention to a woman, much less receive it back. It is the star performers—the wealthy, the famous, the athletes—who receive abundant sexual attention from women. Except for a few men who have achieved enough success, men do not get nearly as much sexual attention from women as women get from men.

Consequently, most men grow up with a huge deficit of sexual loving. They are starving to give and receive it. This striking difference in experience creates a lot of pain around sexual love.

In the paradox of romance and sexuality, our society has sided with romance against lust. In our culture, romantic love media such as romance novels and soap operas are okay, but sexual love media such as sex magazines and videos are shameful and taboo. We glorify the importance of romance, and minimize the importance of good sex. This hasn't worked well. When we side with romance against sex, we find ourselves saying crazy things, like "Sex is very dirty. Save it for someone you love."

Siding with romance against sex has inflamed the war of the sexes. Because men have traditionally been thrust into the role of the sexual aggressor, it is men and men's sexual desires that are publicly shamed when we side with romance against sex. This has created the stereotype that "all men want is sex" when men want sex at all.

The Shaming of Sexuality

Shaming messages about sex often come from people who believe that if something is distasteful and offensive to them, it must be distasteful and offensive to the universe at large. These people learn to despise sexuality in the same way we all learn to despise any part of being human: by having a bad experience with it. For instance, many people are uncomfortable with anger. "My mother was angry a lot, and that hurt me," they subconsciously tell themselves, "so I have learned that anger hurts people. To keep things safe, I will never be angry, and I will try to control people who get angry." Such people have often explicitly decided to never be like their fathers or their mothers, if their fathers or mothers hurt them in some way.

They also have difficulty distinguishing the person who hurt them from what that person hurt them with. If they were hurt with anger, they find anger offensive and have no place for it in their cosmology. It must be eradicated. Instead of honestly saying "I was hurt by anger, I don't know how to handle it, and it really freaks me out," they say "Anger is wrong," or "Anger is bad," or "Anger hurts people." They speak in eternal verities, as if to say, "In God's opinion, anger is bad."

It is as though someone had hurt them with a baseball bat, and from then on they turned against baseball bats, telling everybody who will listen that baseball bats are bad. In truth, however, baseball bats are only baseball bats, and anger is only anger. The appropriate focus of our anger is on the persons who hurt us, not what they hurt us with.

It is the same with sex. Many people—especially but not exclusively women—are invaded by someone else's sexuality at some time. This may happen innocently as in playing doctor, or by overt sexual abuse, or even, for women, by the continuous unwanted sexual attention they get from men. Such abused people have difficulty distinguishing between having sex and being hurt by sex.

Women live in an atmosphere of sexual attention that is difficult for men to understand. It is hard for men, who rarely experience being desired sexually by many women, to understand how painful and terrorizing it can be for women to be constantly desired by men. (The reverse is also true: it is hard for women to understand men's sexual deficit.) A continual stream of sexual attention, with little or no attention to a woman's intelligence, personality, or emotions, sometimes turns sex into a wounded area and an offensive topic. Many women are so burned out on sexual attention that receiving what might be intended by men as innocent sexual attention or interest becomes offensive and frightening to them. Sex, except within a very narrow range, becomes bad, and they label it accordingly: disgusting, addictive, abusive, sick.

People who have difficulty distinguishing sexual trauma from sex itself learn to think of all sex as traumatic. All sexual attention and every sexual portrayal becomes offensive to them. To people with this wound, sexual interest is bad, sexual portrayals in films and magazines are evil and hurtful to women, and men's sexual desires and motivations in relationships are extremely suspect. These judgments arise from confusing who hurt them with how they were hurt. Such wounded people, who are mostly women, attempt to shame others, mostly men, about their sexuality.

Fantasy

It is unfortunate that the desires and fantasies of everyone—women and men—are censored by people who have been hurt by sex. The ability to fantasize and visualize desires is apparently unique to human beings. The range of what we can fantasize, and the variety of possible futures we can visualize, is unlimited. It is this unlimited quality that makes us able to imagine wonderful possible futures—and to make them reality.

Attempting to limit our range of fantasy in any way is a dangerous game. To work properly, our imaginations need to have no limits. This is not to say we should act on those imaginings; we can and should use other aspects of our mind to limit what we choose to do. I can easily imagine stealing a new sports car and driving it cross-country at 150 mph, but I choose not to do it. Business productivity consultants have long known that the best ideas come from people who are allowed to let their minds go, and who are not intimidated into censoring their own ideas before they even have them. Similarly, people function better when they are not intimidated or shamed into censoring their fantasies before they even have them.

When a fantasy is accepted, it is easy to see, and we can make clear decisions about it. When a fantasy is denied, it is harder to see—that is the point of denying it, after all—and it is impossible to make decisions about it. When it starts to come out, we try to ignore it. It has been said that our psyches are like water. If you push what's inside you down in one place, it simply comes out another. Ruthlessly shaming people's imaginary fantasies may only increase the likelihood of fantasies coming out in uncontrolled bursts. People find themselves acting out behaviors they swore they'd never act out again. This was true of a gay man I knew, who tried to repress his homosexuality. He'd push his desires down, and push them down, and push them down, then suddenly lose control, and find himself going to bars, picking up men and engaging in irresponsible and dangerous sexual behaviors. When fantasies burst out after long suppression, they can do real harm to ourselves and others.

For most people, it is not what we desire that causes us grief, but how we have been trained to *feel* about those desires, and the destructive things we sometimes do to *fulfill* them. Again, desire itself is not harmful; it is how the desire is used that can hurt. Yet the stereotype that "all men want is sex" shames men not only for what they actually do sexually—which would be painful enough—but also for what they *imagine* doing. Our stereotypic view blames men for any difficulty with the complex and sensitive issue of sexuality.

Sadly, people who have been hurt by sex are often willing to use shame to impose limits on sexual fantasy, and to inhibit all sorts of sexual expression. Having seen or experienced pain around sexuality, many people, especially women, side with emotional love in a battle against the sexual. Male sex drives and male fantasies are especially hard-hit. The sexual fantasies men tend to have about women and the media that they use to facilitate those fantasies—sex books, magazines, and videos— are commonly judged to be bad, are relegated to the back room, and made difficult to get. When, despite shaming, punishment, and discouragement, men have sexual fantasies and desires, society concludes that "all men want is sex." People then feel justified in shaming male sexuality even more.

Sexual Manipulation

It is difficult to discuss the dynamic of sexual manipulation without appearing anti-sex, and equally hard to write about women's sexual manipulation of men without appearing anti-woman. Still, the system of sexual manipulation that exists between men and women is worth examining.

Men can be and often are manipulated by promises of sexual attention, in much the same way women can be manipulated by promises of career advancement. The power to give or withhold sexual attention is still largely held by women, and men need to learn to recognize when they are being manipulated by promises of sexual attention. When a woman can get special treatment from men by being flirtatious, cute, or helpless, she is using sexual power to manipulate men. If she is wearing especially sexy clothing or making "racy" remarks to get a business deal, she is sexually manipulating men.

Like other forms of manipulation, sexual manipulation relies on the manipulated person's belief in his own helplessness. Because so many men live in such a profound sexual deficit, they believe they are sexually helpless, and thus are easily controlled with sex. But it is easy to claim that "she manipulated me." And it is too easy to accuse women of causing men to lose control over how they behave when women are attractive or sexual. Such arguments of helplessness are familiar from radical feminism. One feminist author, for instance, insists that a woman cannot truly consent to sex with a man, because even if she thinks she is voluntarily consenting, she has been so manipulated by men that she has no power to choose her own behavior. When a woman has sex with a man, according to this argument, she is "eroticizing her own oppression."[93] The argument that men are so sexually oppressed that they must lose control around women's sexuality is as ridiculous as the argument that women are so oppressed that they are unable to consent to sex at all.

Men are affected by women's behavior, and a woman who dresses provocatively should not be surprised or offended when men look at her. But it is up to men to decide how they behave. Men are affected, but they do not have to go out of control.

In sexuality, as in other ways, women and men are more alike than they are different. The claim that we are manipulated by others and have no control over our lives and our behavior is exactly as unattractive coming from men as it is when it comes from women. Just as women are affected when men try to manipulate them, men are affected when women try to manipulate their behavior with sexual attention or implied promises of sexual attention through their behavior, clothing, and other cues. Women need to accept that how they behave will affect how men treat them, both positively and negatively, but—and this is important—*the power to choose how we behave always rests with us*. Some women may try to manipulate men with sex, and they may succeed sometimes, but that does not make men helpless victims. Men can learn to see when they are being manipulated, and to say no to it.

Sexual Security

There is something we can do to heal this sexual rift. We can build the sexual self-esteem and sexual security of both men and women. Just as women can resist men's economic manipulation by becoming economically secure, men can resist female sexual manipulation by developing their own sense of sexual security.

To develop sexual security, we must overcome sexual shame. Many men (as well as women) go through life believing that what they desire is "bad," and that they are "bad" for desiring it. When a man enters an encounter with a woman feeling that there is something about his sexuality that deserves condemnation, he immediately puts himself in a one-down position. This is not women's fault, nor the fault of female sexual teasing. This sense of defectiveness comes from his own shame. What goes on in his mind is his responsibility, and he can learn to identify and change it.

We can change our negative perceptions of our desires by first identifying our negative beliefs about ourselves and our desires. Long-held beliefs about ourselves usually flash through our consciousness too quickly to notice, and we only notice their effects. "Beliefs," says psychologist Martin Seligman, "become so habitual we don't even realize we have them unless we stop and focus on them."[94] Our beliefs become "facts."

For example, Steve is out with Maureen on a date. They have gone out several times, and seem to get along well. At his house late in the evening, he tries to kiss her. She rejects his kiss pleasantly but firmly, saying, "I really don't feel that way about you, you know? I like you, but I want something more."

Steve's beliefs about this rejection probably never reach his consciousness, but if they did, they might sound something like this: "Yeah, I know. Another woman who doesn't want me. Who am I kidding? She can see right through me. I always want women more than they want me. All I want is sex, probably, anyway. My ex-wife said the same thing. I'm not romantic. I just stampede in. No woman will ever want me." This negative self-talk creates anger and shame, which lead in turn to an unpleasant and awkward end to the date. Steve may never call Maureen again, thus ending the relationship.

Things might go much easier for Steve if he could say to himself, "Yes, I'd like to have sex with this woman tonight, and there is absolutely nothing wrong with that desire. She's not interested, and that's too bad, but just because she has a different amount of desire than I do doesn't mean that there's anything wrong with me. My sex drive is healthy, and my desire is a good thing." This internal scenario avoids the awkward shame and anger that Steve feels when he degrades his own desire just because Maureen does not share it at that moment.

Sexual Style

Men can develop sexual security by building their sexual self-esteem. They can learn to pleasure themselves and feel good about it, rather than being wholly dependent on women for their physical and sexual pleasure. They can learn to feel good about what they like sexually. Men can learn to feel good about choosing the kinds of sexual stimulation they want, and can learn to feel empowered in their sexuality.

Furthermore, men can learn to develop their own sense of attractiveness and their own sexual style. Despite some men's macho posturing, many men believe that they are not attractive. This sense of unattractiveness is reinforced by the male experience that it is his level of economic success that attracts women, not what he is himself. This can leave a man feeling hopeless about himself.

When a man's sense of his own attractiveness and lovability depends on sexual affirmation by women, he can only feel attractive and lovable when he is getting the sexual attention of women. This creates a "one-down" situation for the man, because what he needs to feel attractive is outside himself. He is dependent on women's attention to make him feel attractive. He is helpless in the face of their sexual power. He comes to believe that women feel attractive, and are sexually teasing him on purpose (just as women sometimes believe that men's lives are easy, and that men enjoy making women's lives difficult). He becomes ashamed, angry, and emotionally shut down.

Women, too, often put their sense of attractiveness at the

mercy of other women's approval. Thus, men's magazines and women's magazines alike focus on images of attractive women. Men learn they are lovable only if they are having sex with models, while women learn that they are lovable only if they look like models. Although our focus here is on men's experience of feeling unattractive, it is an experience which both genders share.

Men and women who believe they are unattractive can reclaim their sense of attractiveness. Everyone has a personal style, but it is easy to fall into the habit of minimizing or ignoring it. This is unfortunate, because personal style is one of the most wonderful, unique, and attractive things about every individual. Personal style is not trivial. And it does not suddenly appear fully formed. It has to be coaxed out by gradually discovering and allowing what we enjoy and what we desire.

As a man discovers his personal style and learns to live through it, he comes into his real self. He feels better about himself, and becomes attractive to himself. A man who is at home with a well-developed personal style likes his life, because it reflects what is best about him. He likes himself. This makes him attractive to others.

Once again, what we desire is important. Most men are well trained to put whatever they desire on hold until another and another and yet another goal is met. Such men desperately need to start befriending and empowering their authentic personal styles—what they like, what turns them on, what they desire. Men can stop allowing women to dress them, or to decorate their homes. They can learn and empower what *they* like.

Writer Susie Bright encourages heterosexual men to heal their sexual wounds by getting to know and flaunting their erotic style. She says gay men have done it, lesbians are doing it, and now it's time for straight men to let go of their shame for liking sex. "No woman is going to get a better job or walk more safely at night just because you burned your pornographic magazines and announced that sex isn't the most important thing in life," she writes. "Getting laid may not be the most important thing, but sexuality—your desires, your erotic identity—is precious."[95] To feel attractive, we must know what we love, what we care about—in short, what turns us on in life.

An Attractiveness Exercise

It is characteristically human to believe that someone else embodies the qualities we desire. The idea that they have everything while we have nothing leads us to project our sense of attractiveness onto others. This psychological phenomenon is responsible for much of the distance between men and women.

Men (as well as women) can experience the feeling of being attractive through a visualization technique. If I'm feeling unattractive, I can always easily imagine someone who I think is attractive. If I intercept my belief, "She's attractive, I'm not. She's beautiful, I'm nothing," I can put the visualization into action.

Bringing the feeling of attractiveness from her to me requires a little imagination, but anyone can do it. First, I imagine what I think it feels like to be her. I imagine myself in her body, walking down the street. I let my body conform to the posture I believe she has. I let myself think whatever I believe she is thinking. (I may be wildly inaccurate, but that does not matter for this exercise.) For example, I might believe she is thinking, "I'm so attractive. I am beautiful. Everybody desires me." Then, I look for that feeling of attractiveness in my/her body. Where is it? What is its shape? What is its color? What does it feel like? It may be a bright sun shining in my chest, lines of fire going down my limbs, a tiger in my hips, or anything my imagination says it is like.

When I have a concrete metaphor for this feeling of attractiveness, then I slowly let myself return to my own body, *keeping the metaphor and the sense of attractiveness,* bringing it back into myself. I often find that my posture improves after such a visualization, and that I enjoy, at least for a while, the feeling of being attractive *as me.* I have that sun, or that fire, or that tiger in me. Over time, I find that I project the feeling of attractiveness onto women less frequently. A well-developed personal style, and this visualization, can help men and women reclaim their sense of attractiveness, and create a stronger sense of sexual security. Sexually secure men are less likely to be manipulated by sexual teasing, and are less likely to blame women for their feelings of unlovability. Sexual security is worth developing.

Changing Control of Sex

In our culture, women have been empowered in the area of feelings and relationships. Therefore women, more often than men, have the power to judge which motivations for sex are bad, and which are good. Compared to women, men tend to consider more motivations good enough, so women have been able to decide which motivations they will accept. How many men have heard women say "I want something more," meaning some "better" reason to have sex? By contrast, men usually aren't looking for something "more" from sex—their deficit of sexual availability keeps them focused on looking for any sex at all. Many men labor under the idea that part of becoming mature is giving up the hope of getting what they most want sexually. Many a man is willing to sacrifice his desire for good sex, or even to stay in a sexless relationship, because his partner has decided that sex is unimportant, or that it is only acceptable when motivated by some "higher" reason. Her judgment is accepted by the man because they both believe that she knows what is best in the relationship.

Despite our current problems around sex, this is another area in which we have seen a lot of improvement over the past thirty or so years. I recently read the 1962 best-seller *Sex and the Single Girl,* written by *Cosmopolitan* magazine publisher Helen Gurley Brown. I also examined some classified ads from a newspaper of the same era. This provided a perspective on relationship and career opportunities as they existed three decades ago.

The newspaper shows that employment opportunities were overwhelmingly reserved for men, with few options for women. Many of the advertisements began "Man needed to manage…." The limited options for women were clearly spelled out as well. "Girl wanted for…" was common in the want ads of the day, and employers sometimes even stated their preference for married women. Women were clearly held back in business, when they were allowed in at all.

Sex and the Single Girl, a book for women about relationships, shows the other half of the work/relationship dichotomy. Just as men held women back from most career options, women were encouraged and empowered to hold men back from relationship and especially sexual options. "Sex is a powerful weapon for a single woman in getting what she wants from life, i.e., a husband," advises Helen Gurley Brown. While "a married woman who uses sex as a weapon is being a kind of rat,…a single woman who doesn't deny her body regularly and often to get what she wants, i.e., married or more equitable treatment from her boyfriend, is an idiot."[96] Before the rise of feminism, the "love generation," and the so-called sexual revolution, if a man wanted a sexual relationship, his options were basically limited to soliciting prostitutes or getting married. As women's career options have opened up, men's relational and sexual options have expanded as well. As the availability of jobs for women has dramatically increased, the variety of relationships available to men has increased as well.

Between 1962 and 1987, the number of women in the workforce more than doubled.[97] During the same time, the percentage of men of age 25–29 who had never married increased 24 percent.[98] This decrease in the marriage rate may have come about in part because men found that they could get their needs met through other types of relationships besides marriage. Because of the variety of relationships options now available to them, men are less easily manipulated by women's sexual promises than they were in the past. While men still have a long way to go, there has been a great deal of improvement around sexual shame and the control of men through sex.

Accepting Sex

Divesting lust and sexuality of their negative connotations allows us to legitimize our desires and become proud of our sexuality. As long as men are ashamed of the nature, strength, or frequency of their sexual desires, and believe these desires are bad, they will not be able to look compassionately at male sexuality.

The stereotype that "all men want is sex" indicates that many men live in a deficit of sexual love. Looking on the bright side, it also indicates that men pursue sex not because they are low and dirty, but in order to heal that deficit. Healing their deficit of sexual love is a legitimate goal for men. Sexuality is neither trivial nor immature merely because some women may have said so. Our sexuality is something we need.

The stereotype that "all men want is sex" and the belief that men's sex drive is bad are hurtful to men and to all people who want to heal and truly enjoy their sexuality. It is time for all of us to let go of the idea that there is something inherently wrong or hurtful about men and sex. We can start letting go of these stereotypes by simply entertaining the possibility that what we desire is not bad. We can imagine the possibility that our fantasies and desires might actually be okay, or even good for us. We can allow ourselves to enjoy our fantasies a bit more each time they run through our minds. This is one route to healing sexual shame, learning more about our sexual identities, and healing our deficit of sexual love.

Not only must the belief that "all men want is sex" be outgrown. As a society, we must let go of our view that sex itself is somehow dirty and evil, and learn to see sex compassionately. The alternative is to stay stuck in our current social pattern, with women drowning in too much sexual attention, and men left high and dry with not nearly enough.

Although men and women appear to be diametrically opposed around sexuality, men's apparent obsession with sex and women's similar obsession with romance are really only different poles of the same paradox. We can find the middle ground between these poles by developing our perspective on sex. Our society has sided with the romantic pole of the paradox against the sexual pole. By so doing, it has shamed sexuality. Because men usually experience more of a deficit of sexual attention than women do, this taking sides has especially hurt men, whose continued desire for sex has been met with shame, condemnation, and punishment.

The solution is to stop taking one side of the paradox of romance and lust, and to accept and value both sides. We can accept that romantic desire and physical lust coexist in each of us. We can stop projecting romantic desire onto women and sexual desire onto men. We can have a new perspective on sex.

The solution also requires us to develop sexual security and sexual self-esteem. When we have real sexual self-esteem, we can break out of the old power struggles, patterns, and beliefs about romance and sex. When we have a compassionate understanding of both male and female sexuality, we gain a new perspective that allows and empowers both romantic love and sexual love. A compassionate view of sex frees us from having to side with one against the other.

Ultimately, it is the combination of romance and lust, of sensuality and sexuality, that makes our love relationships truly powerful and meaningful. As with all paradoxes, when we can embody both sides, we have access to great freedom and power.

Chapter 8

Beyond the Blame Game

RELATIONSHIPS between men and women have changed. Over the past few decades, women have articulated a new, more compassionate perspective on women. Rude, demeaning, or devaluing behaviors that used to be accepted by women have been called into question. Women have insisted that our society empower them economically and politically, just as men are empowered, and have made great strides. Meanwhile, men have not been developing a new, more compassionate perspective on men. As a result, our society has developed a more compassionate perspective on women, while continuing to believe that men have everything and that men, exclusively, are the problem.

When only one side of a conflict is understood, it is very tempting to blame the less-understood side. This is exactly the trap men and women have fallen into. Having compassion solely for women's experiences, while having little compassion for men's experiences has lead us to blame men as the sole cause of all women's problems and the problems of the world. Because we have not seen both sides, and understood both men's and women's experiences with equal compassion, we have had an unbalanced perspective on gender issues. The war between the sexes has continued to rage.

Focusing on winning, rather than on resolving the problems between the sexes, simply leads to more fighting. Needing to win escalates, rather than resolves, conflict. The more solidly one side takes a stand, the more deeply the other side digs into its position. Resolutions that come from "winning" inter-gender conflicts are always temporary at best, leaving the loser waiting for the next conflict to even the score. While understanding even one side of the gender wars was an important start, to create resolution we must have understanding for both sides.

Compassion and resolution come not from fighting, but from understanding. The solution, then, is for us to marshal our understanding, rather than marshaling our arguments. We must be willing to set our hurts and grievances aside long enough to actually understand the experience of the other gender. When we do this, we create peace in our relationships. We no longer have to fight battles about who's at fault for the problems between men and women. When we compassionately understand the experiences of the other sex, while still having compassion for our own, we move from a way of thinking in which someone has to lose to a way of thinking in which both sides can win. We find innovative new solutions to our differences. We find similarity where previously there was separation. We create compassion where previously there was competition. We are spontaneous in our relationships, rather than having to control them. We no longer have to win at the expense of the other sex. When we have understanding, we win along with them.

Throughout this book, we have created resolution by exploring the less-understood perspectives about power, relationships, stereotypes, violence, and sex. For instance, understanding the different ways men and women are empowered creates resolution about issues of power. Men and women are empowered differently, and our society has only looked at the ways men are empowered, ignoring the empowerment of women. This limited understanding creates distance and conflict between men and women, because we have only learned compassion for the ways women are disempowered. When we see that men experience disempowerment as well, in a completely different realm than do women, we begin to see male and female relationships more compassionately. Men tend to be empowered around goals and women tend to be empowered around feelings. While boys and men are empowered around anything that has to do with achievement— most notably business and politics—girls and women are empowered around relationships, such as feelings, love, and judgments about relating. The ability to be obsessively goal oriented, is the basis of male power in the achievement-oriented realms. Similarly, the ability to be obsessively feeling oriented is the basis of female power in the feeling and relational realms. Seeing both the areas of men's empowerment and of women's empowerment (rather than solely seeing men's power and women's lack of it), creates new understanding and compassion between the sexes. When we see that men and women both experience power and disempowerment, we see that we are more alike than we are different.

A balanced perspective also creates resolution in relationships between men and women. Gender issues are relationship issues, and relationship structures, like business structures, are governed by Deming's 85-15 rule. As we saw in Chapter 3, the 85-15 rule says that 85 percent of problems come from the system under which people interact, and only 15 percent of the problems come from the people themselves. When we blame each other, and look for winners and losers in relationships, we cannot see that the bulk of our problem is the systems of our relationships. We don't see how both sides are hurt by relationship systems.

Furthermore, people who chronically blame their problems on the people they are in relationship with, and who believe that their lives would be fine if only their partner would change, are codependent. Codependent men and women get involved in relationships in which the very structure of the relationship itself creates tremendous suffering for them. Obsessed with blaming the other person for their problems, and obsessed with making their partners change, they are stuck in a dilemma which guarantees that everybody will end up losing. Because the structures of their relationships are 85 percent of the problem, trying to change their partners does not work. Sadly, though, their failure to change their partners only further convinces them of their partners' guilt. As men and women understand the systems of codependent relationships, they become able to change the systems of their relationships and stop blaming one another.

Projection is one of the main dysfunctional dynamics in relationship systems. We forget, or never learn, that the other sex has the same experiences and feelings that we do. When we never learn that men and women are more alike than they are different, we project all sorts of qualities onto the other sex. For example, we project onto the other sex qualities we wish we did not have. If we wish we didn't have anger, we project our anger onto the other sex, and see it in them. If we wish we were never controlling, we project our own controlling nature onto the other sex, and see it in them. We project the parts of us that we wish weren't us onto others, and especially project those qualities onto the other sex.

Furthermore, both men and women project positive attributes onto the other sex. When we decide that we do not have something we desire, then the other sex must have it. For instance, women who find they are restricted in job opportunities sometimes decide that if they are restricted around jobs, then men must experience no restriction in the world of work. Men, too, sometimes decide that, because they have felt powerless in relationships, all women must automatically feel powerful in all relationships all of the time. These projections create tremendous distance between the sexes.

The Rescue Triangle, as described by transactional analysis, is another major dysfunctional relationship dynamic. We fall into this pattern in relationships when we decide that one person is powerful and the other person is powerless. We then have a rescuer and a victim. The Rescue Triangle dynamic starts when we decide that one person is helpless even though he or she actually isn't, and that the other person, the rescuer, is the only one who can help.

Inevitably, the rescuer gets angry at the victim's continuous helplessness. The very helplessness we encouraged with our advice, support, and kind words begins to seem weak, sniveling, and manipulative. We attack, and the "helpless" one becomes a persecutor, and attacks in return. We then persecute each other, and blame each other for the attacks. The fighting has begun.

We create resolution when we see that the bulk of the problems in relationships between men and women are not caused by one of the people in the relationship, but by the system of the relationship. Resolution comes when we understand our participation in the system that victimizes us all. When we see that both we and our partner are being affected by the system of our relationship, we can move beyond blaming. When we understand projection, codependence, and the rescue triangle, we can begin to fix the problems in our relationships, rather than trying to fix blame.

Stereotypes also encourage men and women to see themselves as different from each other, and encourage blame. The women's movement has brought us a new perspective on stereotypes about women, so that people who stereotype women are now often challenged, sometimes quite forcefully. As the stereotypes about women have been dismantled, their inaccuracy has become clear. For instance, it's hard to continue to believe the stereotype that says women are bad leaders when more women are becoming good leaders every day.

This new perspective on stereotypes about women needs to be balanced by an equal level of understanding of the stereotypes that affect men. Once again, if we understand women's experience but do not understand men's, we fall into blaming the less-understood side for the problems of the side we do understand. Because resolution is created when we understand *both* sides of the dynamics between men and women, we explored the stereotypes that still affect men. We looked at "it's a man's world," "all men are alike," "men deserve abuse because men commit the violence," and other stereotypes. We looked at the stereotype that men are always domestically abusive and that women are always victims of that abuse, and at the stereotype that the only thing men are interested in is sex. When we understand these stereotypes, we can understand men's behavior as compassionately as we do women's. We are able to see that men's behaviors come from understandable reasons, just as women's do. We find that people, both men and women, tend to behave like people. When we see that the other sex is human as well, and understand the motivations for their behaviors, we move to a new place of compassion between the sexes.

The "Blame Culture"

When we see men and women with equal compassion, we understand that their suffering and their wounds are similar. For example, we have discussed how men and women tend to have similar experiences in different situations, and how the same wounds are often inflicted under different circumstances for women and for men. We saw that, for instance, while women are more likely to be shamed about what they can or cannot do, men are more likely to be shamed about what they *are:* their morality and value as human beings. We saw how men are hurt sexually through their constant sexual neediness, while women are hurt sexually by the overabundance of sexual attention they often receive. Even though these wounds are inflicted under different circumstances, the shame is the same, and the suffering is the same.

If we see that men's and women's suffering is the same and that our wounds are similar, we have to let go of the idea that men and women are fundamentally different and completely alien to one another. When we give up that idea, we come to the ultimate conclusion of this book. Seeing that we are more alike than we are different ruins our comfortable habit of having someone different from us to blame. If men and women are more alike than they are different, and deserve to be treated with equal compassion, then we can no longer unilaterally blame the other sex for our problems. When we see men and women with equal compassion, and believe that they are more alike than they are different, one of the great pillars that supports our blame culture is swept away.

We have discussed how our culture needs bad guys whom we can blame for our problems. We have seen how, in our culture, the bad guys are almost always men. If we give up blame, we have to give up blaming men. Giving up identifying men as our society's bad guys has serious implications, because men are currently the "designated perpetrators" for almost every recognized oppressed group in the world. When we stop blaming men, we risk giving up our beliefs about who the bad guys are. If we cannot blame men, whom can we blame? It takes some serious psychological revisioning to give up having any all-powerful group to blame for our problems, but seeing men and women as more alike than different requires exactly that.

This one change in perspective can change almost everything we view. The dynamic by which we blame men unilaterally and without compassion is the same dynamic we use when we unilaterally blame any person or group. When we give up blaming men, we open the door for everyone we blame to also be transformed from one-dimensional perpetrators to multi-dimensional human beings. The dynamic with which we blame men is a template for how we use blame in our society. Once we have broken that template, it becomes harder to see a country like the Soviet Union as a purely evil empire, or someone like Saddam Hussein solely as an inhuman monster. It becomes harder to blame another race, another class, another country, or another religion for our problems or the problems of the world. When we see both women and men with compassion, compassion becomes more available for everyone we tend to blame.

Developing this more mature attitude about blame is an essential task both for personal growth and for social transformation. Currently our society embraces blame. We polarize men and women into the roles of perpetrator and victim and take sides, rather than looking for any similarity or middle ground. We try to resolve the war between the sexes by deciding that men are all-powerful perpetrators, while women are utterly powerless victims, or vice versa. This blaming approach never really ends the war; it simply keeps us looking for other people to be bad guys, so we can be good guys. The only way out is to give up having "bad guys" to blame at all, and to end the blame game, forever.

The Risks of Letting Go of Blame

Letting go of blaming carries with it some important implications and risks. Being a victim is difficult enough; giving up being a victim can be even more difficult, because it means giving up the very real benefits we receive from staying in the victim role and blaming someone else for our problems.

We have explored the connection our culture makes between being a victim and being innocent. This connection has created pressure on all groups to prove that they, too, are victims and that therefore they are good people, too. Even men have been caught by this need. A recent *Newsweek* cover story about men, which asks "Are They the Newest Victims?"[99] shows how far people are willing to go to gain the innocence and entitlement of being a victim.

If we give up defining ourselves as victims, we risk that we may not be innocent anymore. If we aren't victims, and don't blame someone else for the problems in our lives, we risk being responsible for our lives and experiences. And finally, if we give up getting our sense of innocence from being victims, we have to deal with the shame we may feel when we realize that maybe we brought some of our victimization onto ourselves by staying in the blaming victim role.

We also risk our motivation if we stop seeing ourselves as victims. Feminist writer Naomi Wolf says, "Feminists often feel anxious when commentators choose to focus on women's achievements, because they fear that publicizing some successes will encourage a return to apathy."[100] As one promotional letter from the *National Organization for Women* warns, "victory cannot make us relax for an instant."[101] Being a victim is a great motivator for change. When we give up blaming, and stop seeing ourselves as victims, we risk becoming complacent and apathetic, no longer motivated to change our lives by struggling to overcome our victimization.

Our fears that we won't be innocent if we are not victims, and that if we are not victims we'll lose our motivation to change and grow, are two reasons why it is difficult to give up blaming. But there are substantial benefits to giving up blame as well.

When we give up getting our self-esteem and motivation to change from being victims, we no longer have to be helpless victims in order to feel innocent. When we no longer need to be victims, we can be more responsible and powerful in our lives. When we stop seeing ourselves as victims we can change and grow, not because someone is oppressing us, but because we are following a positive dream for our futures. When we stop seeing ourselves as victims of someone else, we can build our lives based on what we want, rather than on what someone has done to us. While it is important to know the risks of giving up blaming, it is also important to acknowledge the benefits. When we understand both the risks and the benefits, we can make informed decisions about what we choose to believe.

"But I Really am a Victim!"

Giving up blaming can be especially difficult for people who primarily define themselves as victims. Such people have what we might call a victim identity. Instead of seeing themselves as people who have from time to time been victimized, they see themselves as victims first, and people second. They have great difficulty giving up blaming, because being victims of other people is so intimately connected to their most fundamental ideas about who they are.

Most of us have voices inside us we call "men" or "women," which are actually aggregates of the hurtful things we heard early in life from someone of that gender. We carry those voices with us, and blame them on others. For example, if a man says "Women always put me down sexually," then there is probably a voice in him he thinks of as "women" that degrades his sexuality. He finds real women to play that voice for him, over and over again. If a woman says "Men always abandon me," then there is probably a way she is abandoning herself that she is not aware of. She, too, finds real men to play that role for her. We spend our lives setting up people to play our shaming voices for us, and so see our victimization everywhere, even when it is not really present. Because we do not like to admit that we say such things to ourselves, we look for other people to say them for us. In this way, we can blame those people for victimizing us. When others say to us the shaming things we say to ourselves, we can continue to think of ourselves as victims. People who have victim identities do this continuously, in all areas of their lives.

For instance, as long as a man believes it is women, rather than a part of himself, who shames his sexuality, it is impossible for him to heal his sexual shame without changing all women. As long as a woman believes that men abandon her, rather than seeing how she abandons herself, it is impossible for her to solve her problem without changing all men. If the shaming message is not part of you—if it is women, or men—then you are helpless against it. But if the shaming message is part of you, you can do something about it. We have power once we can admit that some of our victimization comes from our beliefs about the other sex, and from how we use them to repeat our inner shaming messages.

Most people, especially people who have victim identities, also hold on to past hurts as a way of remembering what was lost through some trauma. For example, when I was a teenager, a friend of mine was hit and killed by a drunken driver. I did not drink alcohol for many years after that as a way of remembering my lost friend. In time, it came to seem that if I drank at all, I would in some way be forgetting him, not loving him, or excusing the horror of what happened to him.

People often think that if they let go of their identity as victims they are somehow forgetting or excusing what happened, or are betraying some important memory of their victimization. This dynamic leads people to say, as one woman did, "Once rape occurs, it exists permanently, indelibly burned into women's souls, sights, spirits, sounds, and sexuality. I listen to music as a woman who was raped, I watch television, read the paper and magazines, and listen to the news as a woman who was raped."[102] In our efforts to not forget the horror of what happened, to not forget what we survived, we can let our victimization consume our identities.

I eventually found that I could drink alcoholic beverages and still love and remember my friend. People who identify themselves as victims can learn that they can honor and remember what happened to them without having to live every second of their lives as victims. They can learn that they can be happy and powerful, and still remember what happened to them. We can live our lives as our own, not as the result of what someone did to us.

We can protect ourselves from developing a victim identity by becoming aware of the difference between being occasionally victimized, which we all are, and defining ourselves as victims. To paraphrase Cornel West, director of the Afro-American Studies Program at Princeton University, we have all been victimized at one time or another in our lives. The question is, do we let our victimization have the last word, or don't we? Do we let it run our lives, or don't we? It is our choice.

The Shadow

It can be disturbing to examine the possibility that we have with us a part that clings to being a victim. It may also be frightening to consider that we have within us not only a victimized part, but also a part that is darker in its desires. Yet this is the reality. Carl Jung and his followers called this darker part of the human psyche the "shadow."

The shadow, according to Jungian psychology, is simply the parts of us that we wish we weren't, and that we try to repress. These are the "bad" parts of ourselves, the same parts of us that we project onto others when we blame. This may be feelings, such as anger, that we repress and don't acknowledge to ourselves. It may be desires that we wish we didn't have, like the desire to retaliate when we are wronged. We all have shadows. It is absolutely human. Just as every light throws a shadow, every positive aspiration we have has a shadow which, according to Jung, we must address.

There are risks to admitting to having a shadow side. If we admit to sometimes having the desire to, say, retaliate, or to hurt someone for some reason, we risk that we might be unloving, bad people. This is difficult because it is very important to people to be able to think of themselves as good and loving. We will go to almost any length to preserve that belief about ourselves, including repressing or projecting our frightening shadow parts. As long as we need to be in denial about our shadows to be able to consider ourselves loving people, we will continue our denial.

It is not easy to deny our shadows, though. People who do not acknowledge or take responsibility for their shadows act out of their shadows anyway, only accidentally and without conscious control.

For example, people who have put their potential to hurt others into shadow often hurt others anyway, by acting like victims. Such people often control others through subtle accusations that other people are hurting them or others. They often declare that other people's behavior makes them feel unsafe or afraid, and that the only way out of being perpetrators is for those other people to change in the ways the "unsafe" person wants. One woman wrote about her former roommate: "She was an insufferable control freak. She manipulated by using therapy-speak: 'I feel unsafe.' Everything she didn't like, and there was a lot, made her feel unsafe. Get a grip, girl! How far out around us do we have a right to extend our boundaries? At what point do people have to take responsibility for their own control issues and paranoia, and not expect the rest of us to restrict our lives to take care of them?"[103] People can use feeling "unsafe" to control, and even to perpetrate abuse upon others.

As another example, at one forum about the abuse of women, a woman was booed and hounded from the room because the panelists said she represented a threat to them. One woman there explained that "The panelists are our guests, and you don't challenge your guests when they tell you they're afraid."[104] (However, you evidently do anything they say to keep them feeling safe, even something as mean and unfair as suppressing a dissenting voice at a panel discussion.) By controlling covertly through feeling "unsafe" or "afraid," people dedicated to not being hurtful can hurt others and not even know it.

"This group isn't safe for me as long as there are men here." So all the men leave. "I don't feel safe the way you are leading this meeting." So, to avoid being a perpetrator, the leader changes in any way the "unsafe" person wants. From a victim position, people can control by playing on other people's fears about being perpetrators. Thus they become perpetrators themselves.

Another way to say this is that we become what we hate. When we cannot acknowledge our shadows, we live them anyway, and everyone sees them but us. For instance, many people are quite willing to punish murderers by killing them, because killing is wrong. Thus they become murderers, or accessories to murder, in the way they handle their killer-shadows. Others are willing to condone censorship to stop injustice, thus contributing to the injustice of censorship. Still others believe that all people who discriminate against others should be discriminated against, and thus become people who discriminate against others. The more we try to be people who do not have dark sides, the more we tend to manifest those dark sides in our lives. As one new-age saying goes, "what we resist, persists." Or, in the words of humorist Tom Lehrer, "I know there are people who do not love their fellow man, and *I hate people like that!*"

When we try to be people who do not have shadows, we still have them but become unable to see them. For example, Rebecca is a group facilitator who is very dedicated to her job. She wants to be absolutely certain that every member of her group feels free and uncontrolled by her leadership. By vowing not to be controlling, she puts her controlling side in shadow. Unfortunately for her, the only way she can make sure everybody feels uncontrolled is to control everyone's feelings, overwhelming them with her constant need that they feel free. Consequently, Rebecca is stunned when people tell her that they think she is controlling in the group.

For another example, I once decided that if I were arrogant, I would be a bad person. Consequently I spent a lot of energy making sure that people knew that I was not arrogant. I put arrogance in shadow. Unfortunately for me, having to make everybody know that I was not arrogant put me in the position of having to make sure that people thought the way I wanted them to think. In fact, I treated people as if they were too stupid to make up their own minds about whether or not I was arrogant. The more I tried to make people think I was not arrogant, the more arrogant I appeared.

We easily become what we decided we could never be. One woman, in a conflict with a man, says "I don't happen to have your machine-gun style, Richard, so just shut up!," thus machine-gunning him with the exact same style she is accusing him of having.[105] And for another example, Jane found her first visit to a New York bondage club absolutely detestable. Upon seeing a man whip a woman who was wearing a collar and a leash, she said "It made me angry for days. I would have loved to tie that man up myself. I wanted to smack the shit out of him."[106] Why? Because hurting people is wrong. People who hurt others should be hurt themselves. Through her desire to torture men who torture women, Jane inadvertently discovered the torturer in herself. In this way, angry women can become as repressive as the dominating men they despise, and angry men can become as shrill and committed to being victims as any angry woman. When we repress parts of ourselves, and say we could never be that way, we become what we hate.

As we have seen, ignoring our shadows does not make them go away. Quite the reverse. In fact, when I deny my shadows I become more dangerous, because I become unable to see my dark side when I am acting out of it. For example, if I decide that anger is bad, that anger hurts people, and that I will never be angry, I put anger in shadow. As long as I believe I have no anger, I am unable to see my anger when I am expressing it. I become passive-aggressive. People around me will see my anger, but I won't. If they tell me they think I'm angry, I respond with fists clenched. "That's not possible! Didn't I tell you I'm not an angry person?"

It was only when I admit that I have anger—even though I don't like it—that I am able to begin to get control over it. As long as my anger isn't part of me, there is no way that I can control it. In shadow, my anger controls me. In this way, our shadows, the unacknowledged parts of ourselves, control us.

When Rebecca acknowledges the possibility that she has a controlling shadow, and that she needs people in her group to feel the way she wants them to feel, she is then able to start making changes in that controlling behavior. As long as she won't allow that possibility, she'll never get self-control over her need to control others.

Likewise, I became noticeably less arrogant when I was able to admit that I would do just about anything to get people to think I wasn't arrogant. Admitting that, and not blaming myself as a bad person, enabled me to begin to change those behaviors.

Furthermore, as we acknowledge our shadows in ourselves, we no longer need to repress them when we see them in others. We no longer have the emotional imperative that drives us to get other people to play out our dark sides, so we can punish and blame them, and thus be innocent and pure ourselves. When we can acknowledge our shadows without having to believe we are bad people, we can be responsible for our destructive potentials and dark desires, so other people no longer have to play those dark parts for us. We no longer need to blame them so we can feel good about ourselves. When we acknowledge our shadows, we become more fully human and compassionate.

As we acknowledge our shadows, we become more self-accepting. We can know that having shadows is part of being human, and no longer need to be without shadows in order to be good. We find we no longer need to blame ourselves, or think of ourselves as bad people, if we have shadows. We can be innocent in our shadows, and no longer need to blame others, nor ourselves, for them.

The History of Blaming

To understand how we might finally stop defining ourselves as victims and end the blame game forever, it is helpful to understand the history of blame. Blaming is not static in our culture. Cultural fashions about how we blame have changed, and can change again. According to psychologist Martin Seligman, the idea that human beings can change, grow, and evolve is relatively new. Before the 1890s, common wisdom dictated that you were the way you were; your personality was static, and you lived with it. The self did not change.

That all changed in response to a new idea about human plasticity: that people could change, and could be made to change by their surroundings. This idea, rare in the world before it was propounded by Sigmund Freud and expanded through the work of behaviorists such as B.F. Skinner, said that people are not static, but are products of their environment. Create one environment, and a person will be created along those lines. Create a different environment, and an altogether different person will be created. This idea is fundamentally different from the prevailing thought of much of history, which said that human beings simply are the way they are, and cannot be made to change.

The United States of America is an early experiment to test the idea that people are made into what they are, can change, and can make themselves into something better. America is the land of the rugged individuals, the country of the self-made men. It is the land of rags to riches, where anyone can grow up to be president. The basis of American idealism is that all people are created equal, and have an inalienable right to pursue their own happiness. The United States is founded on the idea that people can make themselves happy. Odd as it may seem today, the idea that people can change or be changed to become happy is relatively new.

Not only do we believe that you can be changed, we have become a culture that believes that you *were* changed to become the way you are. If you are unhappy, you were changed to become unhappy. If you have psychological problems, you were changed to have those problems. You weren't born depressed, or predestined to always have bad relationships with the other sex; something happened that made you that way. Your parents did something to you, or your family did, or women did, or men.

While our society has changed its view on why people are the way they are, our view of blame has also evolved. People used to blame their problems on themselves. If you were poor, it was because you had a moral weakness. If you were an alcoholic, it was because you had bad character. If you were mentally ill and institutionalized, it was because you were defective. There was a cruelty in the punishment of both physical and moral crimes that is puzzling to us today. There was little or no concern for how a criminal became a criminal. Some people were simply bad, and thus deserved whatever punishment they got.

As we learned to see people as changeable, we shifted the blame for our problems from ourselves onto the people who we thought made us the way we are. Much of modern therapy and popular psychology seems bent on assigning blame to the past. Your problems are now caused by your past experiences, or by your family, or by women, or by men.

When people started to understand that they were blaming themselves, and that blaming themselves didn't work, they saw that they could blame in a different way. The way they chose was to blame their circumstances, their pasts, and the people in their lives. Men blamed women, and women blamed men. People found groups to blame, like men, or white people, or economically powerful people.

This is important because it shows that it is possible for our society to change its attitudes about blaming. Getting beyond blaming entirely isn't simply some pipe dream that could never happen. We know it is possible to change the way we blame, because we have done it already. We can do it again. We moved from blaming the self to blaming others. We can move to not blaming at all.

We are starting to see that, as a life-strategy, constantly blaming others for the problems in our lives doesn't work. Although it keeps us from blaming ourselves, which doesn't work either, it also keeps us small, helpless, and confined in a victim-child role. When we see ourselves as victims of someone else, the process of empowerment simply makes us into empowered victims, rather than powerful, responsible adults. Lorenna Bobbit, the woman who cut off her unfortunate husband's penis, is an empowered victim. So are many of the women who kill their abusive husbands. When we define ourselves as victims, empowerment turns into revenge. It makes it difficult for us to change our lives without having to change the people whose fault we believe our problems are. We find ourselves living lives defined by what was done to us, rather than by what we want our lives to be.

The idea of "taking responsibility for your own life" sounds suspiciously like a return to blaming of one's self because, in the past, the only choice we've had about blame has been to either blame other people or blame ourselves. When we have tried to stop blaming other people, we have automatically reverted to blaming ourselves, because that was the only other way we knew. However we don't have to revert to blaming ourselves. We have already changed the way we blame. Our challenge now is to change from blaming others or blaming ourselves to not blaming anyone at all.

When we don't blame others, we can still hold them

accountable for their actions. If someone says they will do something, and they don't do it, they may still need to be confronted.
In much the same way, we must be held accountable in our
lives as well. But such accounting can be done with love and
understanding, rather than with cruel judgment and accusation.
We can be gentle with ourselves and with others. We can
motivate changes with love, rather than with blaming.

A world beyond blame will be a world in which people
are able to look at their own problems, beliefs, and abusive
inner voices without blaming themselves for having them. It
will be a world in which people are able to confront others,
when confrontation is necessary, without blaming them. It will
be a world in which, before declaring war on someone like
Saddam Hussein, the president of the United States handles his
or her own past pain, feelings of inadequacy, or old desires to
beat up the school bully—feelings which could seriously cloud
good judgment—so he or she can do what needs to be done,
and *only* what needs to be done. It will be a world in which
men and women are able to see each other as wounded, noble,
brilliant, and loving. It will be a world in which men and women
are able to ascribe the best motivations to each other's behavior, rather than the worst. When we get beyond blame, the
possibilities are limitless.

Notes

Chapter 1

[1] Steinmetz, Susan, "The Battered Husband Syndrome," *Victimology*, Volume 2, 1977–78, Numbers 3–4, p. 499.

[2] Guisewite, Cathy, *Reflections: A Fifteenth Anniversary Collection*, Andrews and McMeel, Kansas City, MO, 1991, p. viii.

[3] Ibid., p. 131

[4] Clarke, Sally C., *Advance Report of Final Divorce Statistics, 1989 and 1990*, Division of Vital Statistics, National Center for Health Statistics.

[5] Dworkin, Andrea, *Our Blood: Prophecies and Discouirses on Sexual Politics*, Harper & Row, New York, 1976, p. 20.

[6] Robin Morgan, *The Demon Lover*, Norton & Co., NY 1989.

[7] U.S. Department of Justice, *Sentencing Outcomes in 28 Felony Courts in 1985*.

[8] *National Review*, April 29, 1991, p. 13.

[9] *Penthouse*, April 1991, p. 28.

[10] *National Review*, April 29, 1991, p. 13.

[11] *Time*, December 31, 1990, p. 17.

[12] Originally discussed in *The Other Side of the Coin*, Roy U. Schenk, Bioenergetics Press, Madison, WI 1982.

[13] Gutmann, Stephanie, "Date Rape on Campus" *Playboy*, October 1990.

[14] According to the U.S. Department of Justice, the incidence of rape *decreased* 32.5% between 1973 and 1990. *Criminal Victimization in the United States*, 1990, p. 6.

Chapter 2

[17] If you are interested in this concept, and how you can take control of it in your life, you may be interested in the "Inner King Training," put on by Human Development Associates. Call Bill Kauth at 414-823-2586.

[18] Ravitch, Diane, *Youth Policy,* June–July 1992, p. 12.

[19] Ibid.

[20] *Sesame Street Parent's Guide*, March 1993, p. 21.

[21] U.S. Department of Commerce, *Statistical Abstracts of the United States, 1995,* issued September 1995, table 66, p. 58.

[22] Patterson, James, *The Day America Told the Truth: What People Really Believe About Everything That Really Matters.* Prentice Hall Press, Simon and Schuster, Inc, 1991, p. 5.

[23] Ibid, p. 5.

[24] Adams, Scott, *It's Obvious You Won't Survive by Wits Alone*, United Features Syndicate, Inc., 1995, p. 128.

[25] Moore, Robert and Gillette, Douglas, *The Magician Within*, Avon Books, New York, 1993, p. 22.

[26] Moore. Robert, *Masculine Initiation for the 21st Century: Facing the Challenge of a Global Brotherhood,,* text of speech, July 17, 1995. p. 21.

[27] Ibid. Moore p. 22.

Chapter 3

[28] Watts, Alan, *The Meaning of Happiness: The Quest For Freedom of The Spirit in Modern Psychology and the Wisdom of the East,* Harper and Rowe, NY, 1979, c1940, p. 2.

[29] For more on male and female empowerment, see Schenk, Roy, *The Other Side of the Coin*, Bioenergetics Press, Madison, WI 1982, and Farrell, Warren, *Why Men are the Way They Are: the Male-Female Dynamic*, McGraw-Hill, New York, 1986.

[30] Schenk, Roy, *The Other Side of the Coin*, Bioenergetics Press, Madison, WI 1982, p. 130.

Notes

Chapter 4

[31] Dworkin, Andrea, Our Blood: Prophecies and Discourses on Sexual Politics, Harper & Row, New York, 1976, p. 20.

[32] Spicer, Robert, *BallBreaking: The Control and Exploitation of Men by Women*, Amino Books, Australia, 1983. On cover.

[33] Vanity Fair, September 1992, p. 272.

[34] Walton, Mary, *The Deming Management Method*, Perigee Books, NY, p. 165.

[35] Scholtes, Peter R. with contributions by Joiner, Brian L., *The Team Handbook: How to Use Teams to Improve Quality*, Joiner and Associates Inc., Madison, WI, 1988, pp. 2-8.

[36] Wegscheider-Cruse, Sharon, *Another Chance: Hope and Health for the Alcoholic Family*, Science and Behavior Books, Inc., CA, 1981 pp.45–46.

[37] Beattie, Melody, *Codependent No More: How to Stop Controlling Others and Start Caring For Yourself*, Harper/Hazelden, San Francisco, CA, p.14.

[38] Ibid, p. 31.

[39] Ibid, p. 44.

[40] Martin, Judith, *Miss Manner's Guide to Excruciatingly Correct Behavior*, Atheneum, NY, 1982, p. 243.

[41] Ibid, p. 37.

[42] Ibid, p. 16.

[43] Steiner, Claude M., *Scripts People Live*, Grove Press, NY, 1974 p. 146

[44] Ibid, p. 152.

[45] Ibid, pp.152–3.

[46] Ibid, p. 153.

[47] Ibid, *Codependent No More*, p. 70.

[48] Ibid, *Codependent No More*, p. 83.

[49] Pryor Karen, *Don't Shoot the Dog: The New Art of Teaching and Training*, p. 127.

[50] Ibid, p. 129.

[51] Ibid, *The Team Handbook*, pp. 4-20.

[52] Ibid, *Learned Optimism*, p. 15.

[53] Ibid, *Scripts People Live*, p. 153.

Chapter 5

[54] *Playboy*, April 1993, p. 29.

[55] Hite Shere, "Post-modern Masculinity," *Penthouse*, February 1992, p. 101.

[56] Melia, Jinx & Lyttle, Pauline, *Why Jenny Can't Lead: Understanding the Male Dominant System*, Operational Politics, Inc., Distributed by Communication Creativity, 1986.

[57] Op. Cit., *Sourcebook of Criminal Justice Statistics*, 1988, U.S. Department of Justice.

[58] Franklin, Benjamin, *A Narrative of the Late Massacres*, (1763), quoted by Drinker Bowen, Catherine, *The Most Dangerous Man in America, Scenes from the Life of Benjamin Franklin*, Atlantic-Little Brown Books, 1974, p. 183.

[59] "Mothers...had a 62 percent greater rate of violence toward a child than did fathers." Steinmetz, Susan, "Women and Violence: Victims and Perpetrators," *American Journal of Psychotherapy*, Vol. 34, No. 3, July 1980, p. 339.

[60] Barry, Dave, *Claw Your Way to the Top*, Rodale Press, Emmaus, Pennsylvania, 1986, p. 29.

[61] Johnson, Robert A., *He: Understanding Masculine Psychology*, Harper and Row, 1977, p. 1.

[62] *Wisconsin State Journal*, May 14, 1990, p. 1a.

[63] *Transitions*, Vol 12, #3, May/June 1992, p. 4.

[64] The staff of Catalyst, the National Organization Devoted to Helping Women Choose, Launch and Advance Their Careers, *Making the Most of Your First Job* G.P. Putman's Sons, New York, 1981, pp. 192–3.

[65] According to The U.S. Department of Labor, *Employment in Perspective: Women in the Labor Force, Fourth Quarter 1991*, p.1, women now make 74% of men's earnings.

[66] Schenk, Roy U., *The Other Side of the Coin*, Bioenergetics Press, Madison, WI, 1982, p. 109.

[67] *Transitions: Newsletter of the National Coalition of Free Men*, July/August 1990, p. 4.

[68] 1992–3 Student Aid Report, Federal Student Aid Programs, Part 1, Information Summary, p. 1.

Notes

Chapter 6

[69] For more information about violence in lesbian relationships, see, Renzetti, Claire M., *Violent Betrayal: Partner Abuse in Lesbian Relationships*, Sage Publications, Newbury Park, CA, 1992.

[70] *Time*, February 6, 1981, p. 70.

[71] Maccoby, E. E. and Jacklin, C. N., *The Psychology of Sex Differences*. Stanford University Press, Stanford, CA, 1974, p. 426.

[72] Gelles, Richard J. , and Straus, Murray A., *Intimate Violence*, Simon and Schuster, New York, 1988, p. 106.

[73] Steinmetz, Suzanne K., *The Cycle of Violence: Assertive, Aggressive, an Abusive Family Interaction* , Praeger Publishers, New York, 1977, Pg. 89.

[74] Gelles, Richard J. , and Straus, Murray A., "Societal Change and Change in Family Violence from 1975 to 1985 as Revealed by Two National Surveys," *Journal of Marriage and the Family*, 48, 1986, p. 470.

[75] Straus, Murray A., "Wife-Beating: How Common and Why?" *Victimology*, 2, 1977–78, p. 448.

[76] Nisonoff, L. & Bitman, I., "Spouse Abuse: Incidence and Relationship to Selected Demographic Variables," *Victimology* 4, 1979, pp. 131–140.

[77] M. Brinkerhoff and E. Lupri, "Interspousal Violence," *The Canadian Journal of Sociology*, Volume 13, Number 4, Fall 1988, p. 417.

[78] Pirog-Good, Maureen A. and Stets, Jan E., eds, *Violence in Dating Relationships: Emerging Social Issues* , Praeger New York, 1989.

[79] Giles-Sims, Jean. *Wife-Battering: A Systems Theory Approach*. The Guilford Press, New York, 1983.

[80] Mann, Coramae Richey. "Getting Even? Women Who Kill in Domestic Encounters." *Justice Quarterly*, No. 1, March 1988.

[81] U.S. Department of Justice, Bureau of Justice Statistics, Document NCJ-143498, *Bureau of Justice Statistics Special Report, Murder in Families*, July 1994.

[82] Frodi, J., Macaulay, J. and Thome, P.R., "Are Women Always Less Aggressive Than Men? A Review of the Experimental Literature." *Psychological Bulletin*, No. 84, 1977, pp. 634-660.

[83] Gelles, Richard J. , and Straus, Murray A., "Societal Change and Change in Family Violence from 1975 to 1985 as Revealed by Two National Surveys," *Journal of Marriage and the Family*, 48, 1986, pp. 465-479.

167

[84] Stets, Jan E & Straus, Murray A., "The Marriage License as a Hitting License: A Comparison of Assaults in Dating, Cohabiting, and Married Couples," *Journal of Family Violence,* Vol. 4., No. 3, September 1989.

[85] Green, Stanley , Letter to *Newsweek,* August 9, 1994.

[86] These statistics are from a survey, financed by Philip Morris USA in the name of its Virginia Slims cigarettes. Conducted July 22–August 12, 1989, by in-person interviews with a random sample of women across the country. It had a margin of error of plus or minus 2%. This information came from an article entitled "Nasty boys; Women to Men: You Selfish Louts!," *Wisconsin State Journal,* April 26, 1990, p. 1a.

[87] Straus, Murray A., Gelles, R.J., and Steinmetz, Suzanne K. *Behind Closed Doors: Violence in American Families.* Doubleday, New York, 1980.

[88] Steinmetz, Susanne K. "Women and Violence, Victims and Perpetrators," *American Journal of Psychotherapy,* Vol. 34, 1980, p. 340.

[89] Op. Cit. Straus, "Wife-Beating" p. 448

[90] Walker, Lenore. *The Battered Woman,* Harper, N.Y., 1979.

[91] *City Lights,* December 17–30, 1980.

[92] Forward, Susan, *Toxic Parents: Overcoming Their Hurtful Legacy and Reclaiming Your Life,* Bantam Books, New York, 1989, p. 96.

Chapter 7

[93] Jefferies, Sheila, *The Spinster and Her Enemies: Feminism and Sexuality 1880–1930,* Pandora Press, London, Boston, 1985.

[94] Op. Cit. *Learned Optimism,* p. 211.

[95] *Esquire,* October 1991, p. 142.

[96] Gurley Brown, Helen, *Sex and the Single Girl,* Random House, New York, 1962, p. 70.

[97] Women in the workforce:

Women, 1962 19,682,000
Women, 1987 43,142,000
Men, 1962 40,016,000
Men, 1987 54,647,000

From Taeuber, Cynthia, ed., *Statistical Handbook on Women in America,* Oryx Press, Phoenix, AZ, 1991, p. 81.

[98] U.S. Department of Commerce, Bureau of the Census, *Population Profiles*

of the United States 1989, April 1989, p. 27.

Chapter 8

[99] *Newsweek,* March 29, 1993, p. 48.

[100] Wolf, Naomi, "Women As Winners." *Glamour,* Nov. 1993, p. 223.

[101] *National Organization For Women* fundraising letter about the *Political Initiatives Action Ballot,* November 1990.

[102] WISC TV News (Madison, WI), October 10, 1993.

[103] Anonymous letter, Pg. 2, Brat Attack Magazine, #1, not dated.

[104] *Playboy,* March 1994, p.43.

[105] *Ms.,* May/June 1992, p. 55.

[106] *New York Magazine,* Nov. 28 1994, p. 46.

Index

OTHER BOOKS THAT MAY BE OF INTEREST

Negotiating Love:
How Women and Men Can Resolve Their Differences
Riki Robbins Jones, Ph.D.
A groundbreaking, step-by-step program for resolving differences between partners and keeping love alive. Negotiating Love combines male and female communication styles to teach you how to express your feelings together.
Large Sized Paperback, $10.00

Men Healing Shame
Edited by Roy Schenk, Ph.D. and John Everingham, Ph.D., featuring chapters by Robert Bly and Gershen Kaufman
Written by thirty of the top leaders in the men's movement. Never before have such a diverse group of male writers, therapists, and leaders written together and expressed their ideas so clearly. This is an historical work and the anthology to have.
Hardcover, 327 pages, $39.95

Good Will Toward Men: Women Talk Candidly about
the Balance of Power Between the Sexes
Jack Kammer
For thirty years we've heard an articulation of male-female issues primarily from a female point of view. We need to expand the inquiry to include questions such as "who lives happier, richer, warmer, more connected, more fulfilling lives?" and "what is power, anyway?"
Hardcover, 236 pages, $18.95

The Other Side of the Coin:
Causes and Consequences of Men's Oppression
Roy Schenk, Ph.D.
The first book to discuss male shame and women's moral superiority. This unique book explains how men control our economic and political systems, while women control our relationship, morality, values and feeling systems.
Paperback, 383 pages, $10.00

Stick Up For Yourself!
Every Kid's Guide to Personal Power and
Positive Self-Esteem
Gershen Kaufman, Ph.D., & Lev Raphael, Ph.D.
Read this book with your children for time together your children will remember! Stick Up For Yourself! teaches kids how to build their personal power and self-esteem.
Large Sized Paperback, $9.00

We Make the Path by Walking:
Paths from Boyhood to Manhood
Robert Bly

A remarkable introduction to the mythopoetic men's movement. Poet and storyteller Robert Bly uses the ancient Iron John story to discuss male initiation and maturation. Moving and helpful.
2 audio cassettes, $19.00

Pornography: The Other Side
F.M. Christensen, Ph.D. (1991)

Want a new view on a commonly vilified subject? In this well written, well researched book, Dr. Christensen shows how pornography is positive and empowering to both men and women. An important book for people who want to learn a new way of thinking about pornography.
Hardcover, $21.95

Men Freeing Men:
Exploding the Myth of the Traditional Male
Francis Baumli, Editor

Insights into the hearts and minds of fifty-four male authors. Moving and inspiring, this marvelous book challenges our society's most fundamental assumptions about men.
Large Sized Paperback $16.00

A Circle of Men: How to Organize and Run
Your Own Men's Support Group
Bill Kauth

Any man can start a men's support group! A step by step manual (based on 15 years researching 120 support groups), for creating and maintaining a healthy men's group.
Large Sized Paperback, $17.00

HOW TO ORDER

You can order books and tapes by phone, fax, or mail. Simply tell us what books you want and add $2.95 for shipping (in the continential USA, that covers your whole order. Outside the continental USA, shipping costs will reflect shipping rates. Please call or fax for exact figures). In the continental USA and Canada, call toll-free 1-800-203-4028. Outside of that area, call 608-255-4028. Fax 608-251-0658.

In your order, please include: your name; your MasterCard or Visa Number and expiration date, or a check or money order; your shipping address; phone number; and a list of the books you want.

Mail your order to Bioenergetics Press, P.O. Box 259141, Madison, WI 53725.

CLIMBIÉ